Misbehavior is Growth

An Observant Parent's Guide to the Toddler Years

By Amber Domoradzki

Contents

Introduction: Humanizing Toddlers..9
Section One: An Observant Parenting Approach to Toddlers..........29
The Calm Behind the Storm: Staying Patient as a Parent................31
Dealing with the Child's Emotions..45
Setting Healthy Boundaries with Your Toddler 59
Teaching: A Gift, Not a Gauntlet..67
A Child's Fear of Abandonment..77
A Child's Need for Connection 81
Eating Together as an Act of Presence and Love 87
Toddler Conflict Resolution Tools 95
Section Two: Cognitive Milestones in the Toddler Years................97
Introduction to the Toddler Milestones 99
Toddler Milestone 1 – Language Comprehension...........................103
Toddler Milestone 2 – Strings Objects/Events Together...............111
Toddler Milestone 3 – Symbolic Thought......................................115
Toddler Milestone 4 – Memory Expansion 123
Toddler Milestone 5 – Persistence and Insistence.........................131
Toddler Milestone 6 – Decision Making 137
Toddler Milestone 7 – Deliberate Rearranging and Creation.........145
Toddler Milestone 8 – Sequence of Events 153
Toddler Milestone 9 – Creative Problem-Solving..........................159
Toddler Milestone 10 – Abstract Reasoning 165
Toddler Milestone 11 – Budding Morality......................................169
Toddler Milestone 12 – Budding Integrity 183
Future Milestones 195
Future Study..197
Thank you, Reader!..199
Recommended Reading..201
Acknowledgments 203
Works Cited...205
About the Author 209

Dedication

To my husband, Matthew. Your supportive presence, obvious love for our children, and constant growth is appreciated and inspiring.

And to my research subjects, my misbehaving but delightful children: John, Emily, and Henry. Thank you for just being you.

Toddler Rights

Toddlers have the right to…
1.   … be scared.
2.   … change their mind within seconds.
3.   … want to be held, then put down, then held, then put down.
4.   … want Mommy and only Mommy (or Daddy).
5.   … want a *blue* cup not a *red* cup.
6.   … not know the difference between actual scary and fake scary.
7.   … want wildly fantastic things.
8.   … want to help with everything.
9.   … not understand the rules and customs of the adult world.
10.   … go through cognitive growth spurts: the sudden, dramatic cycles of regression followed by great bursts in ability.

Introduction: Humanizing Toddlers

Ah, the dreaded toddler years. Toddlers' reputation precedes them. It is ominous to hear about how children go through the "Terrible Twos." Toddlers have been known to have some flippant, I daresay, irrational, I further daresay, *annoying* behavior.

Toddlers ask for something, and then they don't want it. They don't want to take a bath, and then they don't want to get out of the bath. They don't like the clothes you picked out. They don't want to get dressed at all. They don't want to get into their car seat. They want a *red* cup not a *blue* cup. They want to eat the food you just put in your mouth. They want you to take your head off your body and give it to them. They still want to be carried, but they are getting bigger and heavier. They won't let you move one inch. They don't want you to hold anyone but them. Did I mention the whining? Is it inevitable that these years will always bring frustration?

As a mom, I found that many people had misguided ideas about toddlers' abilities. Strangers would ask if my children, at 18 to 20 months, knew colors, or could answer questions like, "What's your favorite animal?" I read in a book that children can "verbally express their needs by 12 months" (Stephenson). This really isn't true. In the early ones, a child may be able to say one or a few words to express a need such as for "milk," but any parent in the midst of dealing with such young toddlers can tell you that figuring out what they want is not usually achieved via a rational process of discussion. Children don't even start talking fluently until 21 months (van de Rijt and Plooij, ch.11). There is a noticeable language explosion at 18 months and while some children may talk in about four-word sentences while others struggle to say any word, none can really verbalize what they need all or even some of the time. I point this out to show that there is often an unrealistic understanding of toddlers' reasoning capability. This can lead to unrealistic expectations.

Even seasoned parents, I find, have difficulty looking back at this age and remembering what it was like or what worked for them and they readily admit the difficulty of even trying to remember. Everything changes so suddenly that it's hard to remember the differences between an 18-month-old and a 21-month-old—and these two creatures are drastically different!

Based on the work of many authors, I knew that children go through developmental cycles in which, at age-related times, they regress, but after this regression, they show a dramatic burst of new ability. Dr. Brazelton in his book *Touchpoints—Birth to Three* describes:

> Just before a surge of rapid growth in any line of development, for a short time, the child's behavior seems to fall apart. Parents can no longer rely on past accomplishments. The child often regresses in several areas and becomes difficult to understand. Parents lose their own balance and become alarmed. (Introduction)

Dr. Brazelton describes these "predictable spurts in development, and the equally predictable issues that they raise" as "touchpoints." In his book, he describes them up to the age of 3 years. However, as a doctor, the touchpoints listed for the toddler years coincided with his observations of how children changed from their 18-month, 2-year, and 3-year standard physical checkups. Details in between these periods are lacking.

The book *The Wonder Weeks* (van de Rijt and Plooij) describes similar age-related, predictable spurts in development. They call them "leaps." The child, they say, develops a new perceptual awareness during these times. In their book, the authors describe in detail the "fussy period" and the "sunny period" of each leap. Their onset comes at specific weeks over the course of infant development. Their research found ten such age-related leaps in the first 20 months of life, with the fussy period of the last documented leap starting at just over 16 months and ending at just over 17 months.

When I reached the toddler years with my first child, I really wanted more information about natural child development than was available. I thought we did pretty well with my first child, but what kept me alarmed were authors or people who would say things like, "If you don't get a hold of your child when young and be strict about right and wrong, you are going to have a brat!" This gave me a huge complex. How could I know if what I was doing *now* could prevent some awful *future*? And I did not find the advice given to combat this awful future to be terribly helpful. It was usually authoritarian in nature with the generic advice of "set boundaries." The advice was not nearly as nuanced or as thorough as I wanted. I really wanted to know what natural child behavior was and what was not: What part of a child's behavior is expected; what may be a problem of neglect; what needs further coaching, and if some condition does need attention, which techniques are effective? Further, what could I do to develop my child's growing mind? I didn't want just to know that "most things are a stage" and to "not worry about them." I wanted exact details.

The Research

I did not originally set out to do research on toddler mental development. As I went through the toddler years with my first child, I knew to expect age-related stages; I was highly interested in the topic; and I wanted more information, but I did not originally anticipate doing this work. My venture into this happened organically.

I am a stay-at-home mother who homeschools my three children. My approach to education is to take note of what my children are interested in and then provide activities in alignment with their development and interests. Because of these approaches to parenting and education, I kept a detailed journal about my children. I also started a parenting blog called, "The Observant Mom." One of the most popular features of my blog is the stories I tell about how I handle my children when difficult. Because I told these stories to others, I had an incentive to write down in detail the kind of difficult behaviors my children were showing, and how I handled them. Over the course of parenting my first child, I had generated a tremendous amount of detailed observational data about both age-related abilities and difficulties.

When my second child got to be almost 18 months old, which is when I really wanted better answers, I looked through the journals, photos, and stories that I had assembled for my first child. Now, had you asked me if I had a difficult time with my first child, I would have said no. But when I looked harder I started to notice some patterns. "Remember that time when he became annoyingly bossy?" Or, "Remember that time he just absolutely couldn't stand when balls rolled different ways every time someone threw them?" I thought those might be developmental stages, because although the stubborn behavior was noticeably seen, it also dissipated.

I am also part of an online community that discusses these age-related developmental cycles. It is a Facebook forum called *Beyond the Final Leap*. In this community, people would post something to the effect, "29.5 months. I'm going nuts! Is anyone else seeing this?" And piles of other parents would say, "Yes! We see the exact same thing!" In late 2015, I had the epiphany that between my own notes and this forum, I had access to quite a bit of data. I could assemble it into a potential timeline of age-related developmental milestones. So, that is what I did. I posted this rough skeleton, asked if it could be pinned, and asked for feedback. I am very grateful to the administrator of the forum, Zoe Brooks, that she pinned this post.

People immediately stated their gratitude for the research. As I started to fill in details, more and more people confirmed its value and validity. When my daughter was around 20 months old, I realized I might be on to something. It has always been my goal to empower parents with tools to effectively deal with their children. I started my blog because I do so much reading about parenting that I thought it would be very easy to share the insight I was getting to help others. I also have a passion for seeing children be treated well. What could help parents more than knowing what their children's developmental stages were? I realized that this is where my unique talents and other people's needs intersect. I love to take complex systems, behaviors, and ideas, and bring clarity and order to them. I was very interested and enthusiastic about this work. With the feedback from others about its value, I decided to commit to it.

Everything about how I was doing the research became better once I committed—and continues to get better. I took even better notes with my first child, highly detailed notes with my second, I solicited input from other parents, and I added to my library books specifically about age-related development. I have worked with many parents who helped me confirm, amend, and add to this knowledge. A big thank you to everyone who has contributed: without you, this would never have been possible!

After being available and updated for several years, this work has taken on a life of its own. People started using the information I provided. Since I first shared this information in December 2015, some parents have been able to follow along from when their child turned 18 months old until the child reached the three-year mark, which is the age range covered in this book. I include, at each cognitive milestone, feedback I have gotten from others about that particular milestone. A sincere thank you to those who put together statements! Here is but some feedback:

This information [...] has been a LIFESAVER at our house. My first son followed the [Milestones] like clockwork and my second is just heading into this territory now. Whenever we'd hit a stormy period it was so reassuring to know it was all an important part of his development. Lack of sleep seems so much more bearable when you know things will be back to normal in no time. — Beck Fredrickson

I love your work! I always check [your research] when my son is fussy or not sleeping well and so far, you have picked it every time! I share it with girls in my antenatal group too. – Sarah Lewis, about her son Jack

Hi, we are just starting [Toddler Milestone 8], so far, I can see challenges with falling asleep at nap time and night time, understanding, and using today and tomorrow. She remembers things that happened a while back and started making up stories about characters. I wanted to sincerely thank you for documenting all of this, your notes have been so helpful in understanding the developments. – Alexandra LaFontaine

They are just great! So informative and very true to what's going on with my kid to a T! — Katie Blogg, about Toddler Milestones 9 and 10 (2 years, 8 months and 2 years, 9 months)

There are certain approaches to parenting that I believe are critical to doing this research. Much of what I did, I believe, made it possible to do this work.

To a significant extent, I follow The Montessori Method of teaching. I provide stimulating materials and I let my children choose what they want to use. Dr. Montessori writes in *The Montessori Method* that to study natural child development, it is essential to let the child choose activities freely. She compares studying a child who is forced to sit at a desk and do lessons to a child that is allowed to roam as the difference between studying "a glass-covered case containing a number of beautiful butterflies, mounted by means of pins, their outspread wings motionless" or studying live butterflies in their natural habitat. Watching what materials attracted my children and what they could do with them was one clue for me to use in determining where they were developmentally. I could also observe, for instance, if they came back to an activity day after day, showing greater persistence of thought. Being able to see that my children came back to an activity day after day is an example of an advantage that I have due to doing research as a mom, as opposed to a researcher who studies children at periodic intervals for 10 minutes at a time or a doctor who only sees children at periodic checkups. I also strive to teach one lesson per day. I would pick what I thought was an age-appropriate activity and present it to my child. If my child liked the activity, we kept doing it. If they were not interested in the activity, I put it away. This was another clue for me and served as its own form of scientific interrogation. I was at an especial advantage with my second child, as I already had a toy room stocked with a wide variety of learning materials and activities, and she had an older brother to model her behavior after. Having a tablet loaded with educational activities was also very illuminative. I marveled as my children at young ages could, for instance, do The Memory Game.

Another not only contributing, but vital factor in my ability to identify cognitive milestones was that I adopted the positive approach to parenting such that I do not correct or punish my children. Thus, I had a more direct view of what is natural human behavior. Punishment itself can create secondary behaviors. From *Positive Discipline: The First Three Years*, "Punishment may seem to 'work' in the short term. But over time, we know that it creates rebellion, resistance, and children who just don't believe in their own worth" (Nelsen, Erwin and Duffy, ch. 1). Because I did not create "rebellion and resistance," I was better able to identify an irritable period as a likely natural developmental stage as opposed to reactionary behavior.

Using a comforting and non-punitive approach to parenting also helped me identify my children's new capabilities. In trying to get my children to cooperate with me, without using punishment, which is an art and science in itself, I gained much insight. For instance, as I asked my children questions such as "Which shirt would you like?" or "What was your happiest part of the day?" I saw what their answers were, and this served again as its own gentle interrogation.

What was perhaps most important of all in this research, however, was my attitude towards my children. I saw everything they did as exciting and noteworthy. I never saw anything they did as nonsense, wrong, or boring. I would write down what they did, organize the behaviors based on when they were clearly in an irritable period, and then simply ponder it. I often felt like a detective solving a mystery as I laid out pictures and stories of my children clustered by age and tried to find patterns. For instance, when I noticed that my daughter could actively look forward and backwards in a book while trying to find something, and at the same age, she was able to answer the question "Do you want to walk up the stairs or have me carry you?" I knew that she was capable of making a deliberate decision—of consciously choosing one course over another. And so, this milestone I named "Decision Making" (Toddler Milestone 6, 2 years, 2 months). Finding patterns such as this is the heart and soul of this work. As I am with my children at all times, I could look at every activity they did—every lie they told, every time they refused to go to bed, every story they made up—as clues. A stay-at-home mother who homeschools is at a great advantage to do this work.

In addition to this, in which I have documented my own children in detail and attained feedback from other parents, I have cross-referenced my research with others' research on this, wherever it existed.

Summary of Results

This book contains the milestones that I found for children between 18 months and 3 years of age. Numbering for these Toddler Milestones starts at 1, and in future work, numbering will again start at 1, such as for Preschool Milestones. The toddler ones are:

No.	Age—At Its Most Irritable	Name
	Toddler Milestones	
1	18 months, 1 week	Language Comprehension
2	20 months	Strings Objects/Events Together
3	21 months, 3 weeks	Symbolic Thought
4	23 months	Memory Expansion
5	2 years, 1 month	Persistence and Insistence
6	2 years, 2 months	Decision Making
7	2 years, 4 months; 2 years, 5 months	Deliberate Rearranging and Creation
8	2 years, 7 months	Sequence of Events
9	2 years, 8 months	Creative Problem-Solving
10	2 years, 9 months	Abstract Reasoning
11	2 years, 10 months	Budding Morality
12	2 years, 11 months	Budding Integrity

My research shows that rocky developmental stages occur all throughout the toddler years. At age-related times, toddlers become irritable (and whiny and possessive and a host of other behaviors), and then after (and also during, in sputters) this irritable period, they demonstrate a burst of new ability. To differentiate my work from all others, I call these periods of growth cognitive growth spurts. Formally, I identify them as "Milestones."

If you had the right diagnostic tools, at these irritable times, you could see in the child's brain where the growth is happening. During these times, it might help parents to think of their children as having the words "Under Construction" written right on their child's forehead. At its onset, it seems to feel scary and disorienting to the child, and in some ways they regress. I use the term "regression" with slight hesitation: Some of the behaviors do seem like "regression" in that they become

15

incapable of doing something they previously could do. Other behaviors are not regression such as how they have a higher need for connection. "Regression" does not cover all of the behaviors, nonetheless it describes some of the behaviors. Other behaviors seen are they may become clumsy or just start tripping a lot, as if they lose coordination of their body, or they may seem to be in disbelief of what is in front of their own eyes. This initial phase of development comes with irritating behaviors too, like crying a lot, becoming jealous, and so on. But on the other side of this irritability and regression is a new ability. It happens like this with irritability followed by a new ability in a repeated way.

In my opening to this introduction, I had posed the question as to if it is inevitable that the toddler years will bring irritable behavior. The answer is a resounding yes. What I want to show is that odd and irritating behavior is a natural part of human development. It is *biologically inevitable* that this will happen. My joke about this is that there is something in a child's DNA from conception dictating that "At two and a half years old, I am going to annoy my parents!"

Typical behaviors found during the irritable periods in the toddler years are the behaviors that toddlers are already infamous for: meltdowns, possessiveness, bossiness, etc. What I want to show with this research is that there is order in that chaos. The fussiness comes, typically crescendos, stays intense for a while, dissipates, then starts all over again in a predictable, cyclical manner. And there is a reason for the irritable behavior: growing the human mind seems to be a scary and disorienting process for the child. A child changes dramatically from 18 months to three years. Eighteen-month-old children are just beginning to have a language explosion, i.e., they aren't talking much yet. At this age, they have but limited vocabulary, and they do not hold on to thoughts for very long. At Toddler Milestone 5 (2 years, 1 month), they go through a major cognitive spurt, which I called "Persistence and Insistence." At this age, children hold on to thoughts longer, including what it is they want. They also develop big, heavy emotions. At Toddler Milestone 6 (2 years, 2 months), the child reaches the milestone of Decision Making. A child at this age can make a deliberate choice about which course of action might be better. Thus, I consider it the first developmental stage at which reasoning capability is present. After this, their reasoning capability advances greatly. By the time children are three, they have a vivid imagination, can deal with issues of right and wrong, can collect themselves emotionally, be involved in planning short-term future events, and might know which way to go when riding in a car. That is an enormous amount of growth. And it happens in seismic shifts, each one starting with a child who becomes difficult to deal with.

When I look at child development, I marvel at how extraordinarily efficient it is. It takes humans 20 years to develop to maturation, whereas it takes most other animals only a few years, if that. This seems like a long time, but considering what a feat it is to grow the human mind, 20 years is rapid speed. The motto of human maturation, if I could give it one, is "Why waste time not growing?"

Impact on Parenting

I contend that knowledge of cognitive milestones in the toddler years is critical for parents in order to aid their child's healthy development. The child starts to grow in major ways including budding reasoning ability, first conscious emotions, and beginning ideas of right and wrong. How toddlers are handled matters profoundly. How can one deal with this? By having a more detailed blueprint of child development so many more answers become possible. Knowing what you are dealing with allows you as a parent to develop effective tools, methods, and approaches. This is exactly what I want to help you accomplish. My goal is to be like a friendly tour guide—a guide about child development—and offer approaches that allow you to survive these cognitive growth cycles, and then use them to thrive.

In Section Two you will find expanded descriptions about these milestones as well as parenting tools and ideas to use. Section One outlines the parenting tools and ideas. As related to parenting, in Section Two, I include for each milestone four things: details about the irritable period, details about the new ability period, conflict resolution ideas, and activity ideas.

The first item I can provide for parents are the details about the behaviors seen during irritable periods. It's one thing to know that "most things are a stage"; it's better to know exactly what to expect. For instance, at Toddler Milestone 9 (2 years, 8 months) children become seemingly paralyzed. As one possible way that this can materialize, there might be a toy that is two feet away from them, and they scream for it but won't get it. Certainly, this can annoy parents. ("Just get it! It's right there!") But if you know that this happens, you will be prepared for it. You can think about how to handle it, thus be better able to respond to it and not blindly react.

For me, I was able to reframe my attitude towards the irritable periods and sometimes even my schedule when I knew one of my children was in one. At Toddler Milestone 6 (2 years, 2 months), I found the child might start to play jokes. My daughter for instance kept hiding spices from me as I tried to cook. At first, I was annoyed by this. I think I may have even yelled "I don't have time for games!" When I figured out it was part of her development, I went from "I don't have time for games!" to "Oh, it's a game. It's cute." At Toddler Milestone 2 (20 months), I was at first in disbelief that another one was happening again only a few weeks after the last one had ended. When I figured it out though, I cancelled all plans for a week to deal with my toddler who kept demanding I hold her. And it turned into a lovely week for us! Up until that point, I had trouble bonding with her. But after that week, we were very bonded. What could have been a negative instead became a positive. Toddler Milestone 12 (2 years, 11 months) was really trying for me. I was not able to cancel all plans like I wanted to as I then had an infant son. Though I desperately wished someone would take one (or three) children off of my hands for a bit, that wasn't an option. Once I accepted this reality, I was able to reframe moments over the course of the week it took to get through the hard part. I made the conscious decision that at some points chores would not get done, and my entire day would be simply dealing with my toddler. At all times though, knowing what was happening helped me cope with it, and it helped me go towards my child, rolling with and even finding joy in these challenging times.

I'm not saying that these rocky developmental stages are easy. I will never diminish how hard these periods can be, but understanding them and reframing the child's behavior can help. The behavior can still annoy parents, and from my reading, very few parents are immune to irritation. Just knowing that these occur can calm a parent's fear down, but knowing exactly what behaviors you can expect is sure to be immensely powerful. The irritation which can otherwise consume a family might be brought down to at least manageable levels.

The second thing I can provide are details about the new abilities seen. My research of the cognitive growth spurts found that many of them had a dual nature between the irritable period and the new abilities period. The thing that children regress at is often the very thing they are about to show great progress at. For instance, children do become paralyzed to solve their own problems during the irritable period of Toddler Milestone 9 (2 years, 8 months), such that they, as mentioned previously, won't get a toy that is right next to them. However, in the new ability period they become very good at solving problems. They might go outside, see it's raining, and verbalize the following, "Oh no. We have a problem. It's raining. What can I do about this? I'm thinking about it. I know! I'll get an umbrella!" I called this milestone "Creative Problem-Solving." In the irritable period, they won't move to solve a simple problem (regress), but in the new ability period, they can solve a complex problem (progress).

I found this was how cognitive growth spurts often went: Children misbehaved before they behaved. They become paralyzed to solve a problem before they become confident; they become bossy before they show gratitude; they knock towers over before building them carefully. I use the term "misbehavior" loosely. They are indeed simply experimenting, and/or their brain is in temporary regression. Children are not being intentionally naughty. But you'll know what I mean when you get to it. It's the stuff that can really irritate and cause frustration. They seem to be out of control and destructive. But if one understands this general cycle, it can have an enormous impact on parenting. What they seem so bad at is the very thing they will soon get good at. And by bad I don't just mean "struggling." I mean *aggressively bad* at. It's those moments that might make you want to yell "Oh my! You just did that on *purpose!*" But if you can just hold on during that bumpy ride for a bit, at the other side of it is a light of hope: You'll have not just a calm child, but one with a new ability which they can use for productive and helpful ends. If you can handle with care the toddler who grabs knives by the blade, gets into the toothpaste, demands you not move one inch, keeps tripping and falling, and whines a lot, you'll soon see a child who is helpful, competent, and coordinated. What I just described, by the way, is Toddler Milestone 11 at 2 years, 10 months.

To deal with this bumpy ride and other situations, for each cognitive milestone, the third thing I provide is a section on conflict resolution. In this section is how to deal with behaviors or situations that are irritating or difficult. It is dealing with those behaviors that others may see as "bad." Many would use punitive measures to handle these situations. Because the problem arises not due to any character defect of the child but the bigger situation itself—their developmental stage combined with having to conform to adult expectations—I entitled this section "Conflict Resolution" instead of "Discipline." The issues that arise are issues of conflicting needs among the people involved. In this section I will discuss how to handle situations where you need your child to respect you, respect material things, be safe, get into car seats, and so on. Any situation where the need of another person (or the toddler themselves) is in contradiction to the immediate whim of the child.

My approach to conflict resolution is to get your needs satisfied as a parent and have the needs of the child satisfied as best as possible, and to have situations go as smoothly as possible. I fight nothing. If I find myself in a battle with my child, I stop myself and think of what a better approach could be. I have read many books on discipline and conflict resolution from experts who weigh in on the issue. Most advice is picked up from these experts, who deal with children as therapists or teachers day in and day out. My approach is a little different from others as applied to toddlers as I take ideas from a host of thinkers about conflict resolution—the first step of which is empathetic listening—and I push them to the toddler years as best can be done. In this way, the child is treated as a respected individual in the family. It is modeled for them daily what respectful relationships look like. It is effective both in the short term at gaining cooperation and the long term at imparting an ideal skill set.

Because they are not developmentally ready for full conflict resolution however, with its brainstorming steps, etc., modifications must be made for toddlers. Several books discuss positive discipline "tools" to use with children. These tools apply in situations when you need your child's cooperation. The toddler (and preschool) years are very tool heavy. At each milestone I have matched it to the approaches or tools that I think are effective based on where children are cognitively. For instance, why distraction works so well for very young toddlers but "offering limited choice" does not (they cannot be expected to make a deliberate decision until Toddler Milestone 6, Decision Making, 2 years, 2 months), or why using "I" statements is effective starting in the late twos. I designed this book with "Section One: An Observant Parenting Approach to Toddlers" first, which gives tools and ideas to parent and teach effectively such that you are educated on these ideas. Then in Section Two, for each milestone I list the tools that are likely to be effective at that age and why. In this way, as you deal with your child at each milestone, you can go to the exact age of your child and find instant, valuable information. Toddlers change rapidly, and this body of work can serve as nearly a month-by-month guide.

As noted, Section One deals with effective parenting tools and approaches. There are some basics that apply across all ages and without knowing these basics, the exact approaches outlined at each milestone may not be effective. The chapter within, "Dealing with the Child's Emotions," describes a critical step of conflict resolution, which is dealing with the child's emotions. Children must be in emotional comfort before you appeal to whatever reasoning capability they do have. The overall atmosphere must be one of emotional comfort, otherwise none of the advice will work. Understanding how to deal with children's emotions becomes vital at Toddler Milestone 5, Persistence and Insistence, 2 years, 1 month. Big, heavy emotions set in at this major milestone and must be dealt with. I also include a chapter on "Setting Healthy Boundaries with Your Toddler." In this, I discuss typical core conflict resolution principles such as defining who owns the problem and how to respectfully state your concerns to a toddler. Starting at Toddler Milestone 11, Budding Morality, 2 years, 10 months, also a major milestone, a toddler becomes able to understand "I" statements as well as other reasoned, well-stated concerns, of which this chapter can help you articulate to your child well. I include also a chapter on "Toddler Conflict Resolution Tools," which summarizes every tool that may appear in Section Two.

Perhaps the most important of all tools is a parent's patience. A wise woman told me once that if we can handle our own emotions, a reasonable enough solution usually follows. Dealing with children who are in the midst of an irritable period is difficult. It wears on a parent's patience (or any other caregiver). The chapter "The Calm Behind the Storm: Staying Patient as a Parent" is dedicated entirely to managing your own emotions. In this chapter, I talk about the usual stuff that is recommended, such as taking a deep breath, then I discuss what really works: bringing your own feelings into conscious awareness, which I learned from Dr. Shefali Tsabary. This chapter gives the tools to help you emotionally as you deal with these rocky developmental cycles. I include thoughts and reminders about the principles regarding internal emotional regulation at several of the more difficult milestones. I describe many of the behaviors and approaches to conflict resolution in story format, in which I describe my own struggles, and in doing so I hope you realize that *you are not alone*. I invite you also to join the Facebook discussion forum, "Misbehavior is Growth—The Discussion," to find other parents who can provide ideas, comfort, and understanding as you go through these milestones with your child.

What I have been describing are ways that you can survive the day to day difficulties during rocky developmental cycles. Now I want to talk about how you can thrive. The fourth thing I provide at each milestone are activity ideas. The most important message I want to bring to people is that this misbehavior has, on the other side, a new development, and, therefore, the growth spurts are not simply times of irritation to get through, but *investment opportunities*. Understanding cognitive growth spurts, I believe, engenders a parenting approach that gets away from trying to fix or punish perceived negative behavior and invests entirely in building positive skill sets.

People are already aware of these cycles, which begin with regression. They tend to call them "stages" or "phases." When a child is acting up at an age-related time, a mom might tell another mom, "Don't worry. It's a stage. He'll outgrow it." This is healthy enough advice. It recognizes that these are natural stages of development and the child should not be punished for it—and that they pass. But this advice is then followed up with, "Ignore it. Don't feed the attention." The parenting approach that I am advancing is that this "misbehavior" is more than just a stage: it's growth. Following this irritating behavior will be (the potential for) a new ability. And so therefore, don't ignore the behavior, *lean into it*. See the misbehavior as a code—a giant Bat-Signal in the air—that a child *needs* someone. They don't need punishment or insults. They need connection, guidance, and teaching. There is something growing in them that one can help nurture. This is the meaning behind the title of this book series: misbehavior is growth.

This is already known healthy parenting advice. From *Positive Discipline for Preschoolers*, "In fact, most young children's misbehavior is a sort of 'code' designed to let you know that they don't feel a sense of belonging and need your attention, connection, time, and teaching" (Nelsen, Erwin and Duffy, ch. 1). If you know specifically what the misbehavior is a "code" for with the documentation of these milestones, you can be in so much of a better position to provide it. After becoming aware of the exact details of the cognitive growth spurts, I hope people no longer say, "It's a stage, ignore it." I want them to say, "It's mental growth, invest in it!"

By understanding the cycle of development, I believe any inclination to punish children for perceived bad behavior will all but vanquish. Instead, given the enormous storm inside of them, children need *connection*. The general approach is to love them harder. Children literally cling to their parents during these cycles, and yet somehow the dominant advice up to now has been to push them away. When you understand the cycle, pushing children away seems baffling. Bringing them closer will not reward bad behavior. It models loving behavior and helps them grow in their emotional maturity. I see cognitive growth spurts now as both investment opportunities and love opportunities.

Further, the benefits of investing with activities, teaching, and guidance for your child are many and huge. For starters, it can help calm the child down. Much of their misbehavior is a desire to learn and grow. If you know how they are growing, you can redirect it into productive ends. This has the effect of calming the child, as you are meeting their developmental need. Montessori writes about "normalization." By this she means providing a child with an activity that they are interested in and focus on, which has a calming effect on the child as well as builds patience and an attention span. The better you are at providing activities they are interested in, the more likely that this effect will happen.

> When very young infants are provided with an environment that offers them the opportunity to practice emerging skills, they become more interested in their environment, more alert, and more cheerful. In fact, a basic principle of good child-rearing, especially during the first years, seems to be that you should design your child's world so that his day is rich with options for activities that relate to his rapidly shifting interests and abilities. (White)

The main benefit, however, of investing is to give children a chance to work on the new skills that their new brain structure allows. I want to stress an important aspect about what happens during this mental growth. Children don't necessarily develop a new skill, they develop the *capacity* for a new skill. Children are wonderfully built like wind-up toys who set out to use the new skill growing in them, and they aren't terribly good at it at first. In fact, they are destructive. They have it "in" them to practice the skill by getting their hands on seemingly anything to help their developing minds, but adults can either help or hurt this process.

The Center on the Developing Child at *Harvard University* describes that "Having responsive relationships with adults, growth-promoting experiences, and healthy environments for all young children helps build sturdy brain architecture and the foundations of resilience." Investing in each cognitive milestone with activities doesn't just build a particular skill, it builds the child's very brain structure. I imagine the child's growing mind as like building a bridge, and each milestone is a step in which the steel beams are being riveted on. The purpose of constructing it properly and with care is so that part of the brain can be used well in the future. But the brain, unlike a bridge, is more like a muscle and therefore it grows optimally through *use*. Giving a child a chance to flex their brain "muscle" and build neural pathways helps provide the lifelong benefit of how to think. You give your child the chance to develop some part of their brain at its most optimal time.

Another important aspect of mental growth is that each milestone doesn't necessarily open a new potential that stays open. Each milestone opens a sensitive period, which is a window of opportunity for building a skill. These periods open but also eventually close. For instance, it is commonly known that if a child doesn't learn to speak when they are young, they will have great difficulty learning to speak as an adult, because that sensitive period has shut down. These periods are thankfully wide, but they do end eventually. If we know what skill is being built at what time, we can unleash a huge potential.

I found that the abilities developed over the course of these milestones cover the full gambit of those skills required to thrive as an adult. It is too often the case in formal education that education means only learning "practical" skills while the emotional, social, and moral development of the child is neglected. Understanding cognitive growth spurts can help with academic skills, but it can also help with these other aspects of human development. It's an education for all that makes one a human. I thus want to highlight the growth of a moral skill as seen even in the toddler years: In the late twos, children start to develop abstract ideas of right and wrong. It is very simple at this age such as, "It is better to not spill milk," but this is a great opportunity to invest in some simple lessons about right and wrong and to start modeling healthy conflict resolution. From personal experience, this had an extraordinary effect on our family and helped keep our house calm. For instance, I once successfully convinced my toddler to stop hitting me by using a well-constructed "I" statement. Modeling this also imparted impressive conflict resolution skills to my children, which I have observed in my older child. This shows how investing in cognitive spurts can have both immediate and long-term benefits.

It also demonstrates how it is possible to teach a child right from wrong without using punishment. Knowing when a child's mind is ripe to receive a lesson about right and wrong is a much more effective approach to teach ideal behavior than physical, emotional, or social trauma (respectively: spanking, yelling, and punitive timeouts). A heart-to-heart discussion at the right time goes a lot further than a punitive measure. And you can reap the rewards of your efforts almost immediately as you notice markedly improved behavior. This—investing in character and mind-building activities, not punitive measures—is how a child becomes disciplined.

Teach by teaching, not by correcting. — Dr. Maria Montessori

Certainly however, understanding cognitive growth spurts can help with academics and specific skill sets. As but one example, I taught my second child to read by the time she was three years old. She could read simple Consonant-Vowel-Consonant (CVC) words such as "cat" by sounding them out and she could use context clues to figure out words, even sentences.

Understanding the cognitive capabilities of my child helped to develop highly age-appropriate lessons. I outline at each relevant milestone the activities I did towards this end. Many of the activities are either Montessori or Montessori-inspired. I was able to take many of Montessori's activities and divide them into highly specific ages at which they apply, and why. You will find many activities that develop a sensory education with simple step-by-step directions that will develop visual acumen, fine motor skills, observational skills, and creativity. I also have lessons related to mathematical, navigational, and reading comprehension skills. Truly, these lessons can unleash the enormous mental power in children.

I found that the process of learning, whatever the skill involved, when done with deep respect for natural child development, was a joy instead of a burden or fight. It was also extraordinarily efficient. Knowing what activity to provide at what age, when they are hungry to work on their new developing skill, allowed for simple, quick lessons that were easy to give and well-received by the child. Many of the activities that I present, especially at these young ages, can be done right before the child goes to bed.

Because presenting activities does require some understanding of teaching, I also include a chapter for parents on basic teaching skills entitled "Teaching: A Gift, not a Gauntlet." Quality teaching is not hard, but there needs to be a reversal in the way many adults approach it. My experience is that many adults are overbearing, ask too many questions, "sermonize," and try to direct their child's learning too much. I learned how to teach young children by reading many books by Dr. Maria Montessori, some of them twice. She advocates a teaching style which relies on simple, strong demonstrations, few questions of the child, and putting away activities if the child is not interested. I focus on developing lessons that are conceptually clear for the child, also explained in this chapter.

The chapter on dealing with emotions, "Dealing with the Child's Emotion," is also relevant to teaching, because a child in emotional distress is not in a position to learn. The big emotions need to be dealt with first. The child needs soothing if they are upset before giving any lesson whatsoever, including lessons on ideal behavior. Many approach the child with the paradigm, "I'll let you be comfortable after you learn or behave." The approach outlined below is, "Make the child comfortable, and then they'll learn and behave."

I find educators tend to fall on one side or the other of a dichotomy where they value teaching skills *or* valuing the emotions of students. On the "teaching skills" side are people who value performance and do not care if the child's underlying emotions are handled well. On the "valuing the emotions" side are people who highly value the child's emotions but sometimes dismiss teaching skill sets, because they think that the instruction will necessarily be abrasive to the child. My work on cognitive developmental milestones should help unite anyone who is on either side of this usual skills/emotion dichotomy. Cognitive growth spurts come at first with big emotions, end (potentially) with major skills, and knowing the cycle of them will naturally allow adults to support the child when they need support and challenge the child with advanced activities when they are capable. In fact, already established healthy parenting principles—embracing "growth mindset," handling negative emotions well, seeing misbehavior as a code for further connection, brain neuroplasticity, providing stimulating activities, interest-led learning, not correcting or punishing a child—are taken to the next level by understanding the cycles of cognitive growth.

I fundamentally trust the process. I believe all education should be designed around which cognitive milestone a child is at. It should be bottom up, child-centered, not top-down, dictating a certain curriculum. I imagine child development like a river, and the cognitive growth spurts are represented by waterfalls. I see many education and parenting styles as fighting the river. When the river is fought, bad things happen. Anything that communicates, through punishment or words, to the child *"There is something wrong about you"* is harmful. The child feels like there is something wrong with them, causing that piece of them to wilt and die; education becomes a drag, and parenting becomes a never-ending battle. It doesn't have to be like this. If we know the course of the river and just *accept* it, while it can still be a tumultuous ride, it is much more navigable. It can even be fun, like white water rafting, as one immerses themselves completely inside their child's world. Looking at the world through a child's eyes is an adventure as they look at the world with great curiosity, vivid imaginations, and startling observations. If you tap into your child's inner teacher, you will see that they have boundless energy for pursuing activities and challenges. It is no longer a fight to get them to learn or behave.

I personally always felt behind at each milestone. I felt there were many activities that I could have provided, but there was never enough time and I never had enough knowledge to teach all I wanted. My children eagerly anticipated the activities I provided. I see each milestone as like a springboard. It's an opportunity to catapult up to a new level of greatness. My vision is that, in the same way that the human genome was mapped, all cognitive milestones will be mapped.

I wrote earlier about people who warn you that you'll have a brat unless you are strict with your child at an early age. I unequivocally reject that, and here is my counter: If you are but *present* with your child, especially at each cognitive milestone, you can be practically guaranteed that you are providing your children what they need. Dr. Tsabary writes that the problem between parents and children is a difference in "time zones." She writes in *The Awakened Family*:

> In fact, were you to ask me what I believe to be the root of conflict between parents and children, I would tell you that it's a clash of time zones. Parents are oriented to the future, to getting to wherever they imagine themselves to be going. Children, on the other hand, when left to themselves inhabit the present. (ch. 2)

I am with Dr. Tsabary: We can be simply present, and connected, with our children, and trust that our children have endless creativity and resources in them to succeed later. A parent's main job is to guide their child's growth as they go on *their* journey, but being this guide is enormously powerful. A parent does not have direct control over the exact outcome of their child; they have but tremendous influence.

Ultimately, proper parenting is the presence of *love*. I see understanding cognitive growth spurts as the ultimate love: understanding something going on inside your child that they have no hope of ever communicating to you, which comes across in such irritating ways, and yet still meeting this deep need of theirs with patience and wisdom.

This work serves to humanize toddlers both by identifying as natural the swirling storm inside of them and by illustrating the amazing capability of their growing minds. A child who is always calm is a pipe dream. It will never happen. At the same time, their potential is enormous. Toddlers are not dolls that can be put away, but living creatures with major, rocky, awesome transformations. This work can humanize you too as you deal with these inevitably difficult changes.

I named my blog and website "The Observant Mom" and this book "The Observant Parent" because I found all good parenting begins with observation—much like a doctor who evaluates, with competence and compassion, his or her patient as he or she decides what course of action to take. The fundamental component of quality parenting is to take children's cues, signals, and statements into consideration as one makes parenting decisions. When they are infants, a parent can look at their hunger and sleep cues. When they are toddlers, a parent can begin to take into consideration their emotions and words as well. Understanding these cognitive milestones will be one clue to the puzzle of understanding children. What I propose is that quality parenting comes down to *thinking*. When a parent brings their emotions into conscious consideration, they are thinking about them. When a parent identifies their children's emotions for them, you help raise their awareness of those emotions—a cognitive process. Comparisons between healthy and unhealthy parenting models might be thinking versus blind reactivity; loving versus authoritarian; connected versus irritated; observant versus negligent; present versus absent. I hope you find value in this book as you adopt the role of observant mom, dad, or caregiver of any sort and put together the clues about the child you have the privilege of helping raise.

I hope after reading this book you feel like a mom, dad, grandma, grandpa, aunt, uncle, family friend, or caregiver of any sort, who is in control of yourself, who is confident in handling toddler meltdowns, who can effectively get a child to cooperate with you, who makes repair attempts when things go wrong, who knows how to give positive lessons to maximize your child's learning, and who is inspired to keep advancing your own skill set. The themes of this book are presence and *growth*. What I hope to do is minimize the frustration that toddlers bring to a manageable level so that what is left is your child with his or her unique talents and interests.

High five, Mom and Dad. You got this!

Section One: An Observant Parenting Approach to Toddlers

The Calm Behind the Storm: Staying Patient as a Parent

A wise woman once told me that the most important thing you can do as a parent is to keep your emotions under control. If you can do this, you can find a reasonable solution to most problems. A central goal of this book is to give parents a set of tools they can use with their children. To be thinking about what to do and not simply reacting, emotions, your emotions, need to be managed in a healthy way.

However, this is much easier said than done. There are few things on earth that can push a person's buttons like children. I thought I was an eternally patient person—until I had kids. I found I was lacking in emotional regulation skills as I tried to deal with my children and, so, I sought out guidance.

I found that for parenting, traditional advice just doesn't work. Some advice might be, "Take a time out in another room." But if you have children who are attacking each other, you have just spilled coffee all over your laptop, or you are the target of many other circumstances, leaving the situation is impossible. Most pressingly, a parent often must make decisions within *seconds* and must do so immediately after just becoming enraged over something. It is possible to go from complete calm to complete enragement in a matter of seconds when you have children. This is very much unlike dealing with adults, where situations tend to escalate slowly. And, these are your kids! It's one thing to blow up in an incidental encounter with an adult (though I don't recommend this); it's another to blow up on your own kid. And parenting is 24 hours a day, 7 days a week. It cannot be overstated: although it is a herculean task, staying calm is vital.

I personally found much of the advice in parenting books about how to keep parental emotions in check to be either highly judgmental or ineffective. Many authors clearly disapprove of impatient or grumpy parents—good parents, somehow, magically, have an eternal supply of patience. Said authors may lecture parents to budget their time better or hire more babysitters as a solution to help stay calm. In other words, they provide no new knowledge or skill sets to deal with parental frustrations. They expect parents to do more with the same amount of time, money, and support: Just try harder, budget wiser, shake the couch to find some more pennies. It's patronizing to anyone in the trenches, to say the least.

Empathetic advice to parents comes from Dr. Ginott. I deeply appreciate that Dr. Ginott, his students, and several other authors discuss how overwhelming parenting can be and that few parents, if any, are always calm, patient, and rational. It is good to know that you are not alone and to know that if you make a mistake, you can work to rectify the situation. It doesn't mean the end of you as an otherwise excellent parent.

Everything said, I did find some problems in the advice from the good doctor about how to stay calm. He says it is allowable to say something like this:

> When I see the shoes and the socks and the shirts and the sweaters spread all over the floor, I get angry, I get furious. I feel like opening the window and throwing the whole mess into the middle of the street. (ch. 2)

For me, the problem was that I found *saying* something like this lent itself too easily to *doing* it. In defense of Dr. Ginott, this advice is meant to be employed only after milder attempts have been made to deal with how angry you are. The problem with this approach, however, is venting anger itself. I find that anger spins out of control easily. Modern advice about anger (discussed later) typically tells you *not* to vent anger. It's acceptable to vent other non-threatening feelings, but venting any emotion where you want to lash out is dangerous. I wouldn't recommend allowing yourself this explosive option unless you have extensive practice with other anger management skills first.

The following are tactics to stay calm as a parent, such that you can stay calm, in control, and present as the parent you want to be during maddening moments. I list some of them as the solution, for instance, "Taking a Deep Breath." In others, I list identifying the problem, such as "Mom Brain." I did this because I find stating a solution, when a problem feels overwhelming and consuming, can sometimes feel like a lecture and, thus, patronizing. Sometimes what is needed is to recognize the problem and to have someone identify it and just sit with you and empathize. When someone does this—identifies the problem and stays there for a while—it can lead itself naturally to solutions. So, some of these tactics list the solution, some list the problem, and I do this on purpose.

Take a Deep Breath

Because several parenting books were rather weak on the subject of parental anger, I picked up a book specifically on anger management, *Healing the Angry Brain: How Understanding the Way Your Brain Works Can Help You Control Anger and Aggression* by Ronald Potter-Efron. The author designed his book for people with terrible anger problems, which is not most parents, but it describes a few fairly effective tools that I applied to parenting situations.

The book's best tool was deep breathing. Potter-Efron explains that there are parts of the brain responsible for getting excited and other parts responsible for calming down, and the two cannot be on at the same time. Taking a slow, deep breath, counting to four and back again as you do it, is a powerful way to calm the body down *instantly*. This works for a parent as a very powerful tool that requires no extra resources to employ and that can be employed in those few crucial seconds available to you. A deep breath—a count of 4 in and a count of 4 out, if you can remember it—can help block you from a regretted action.

Potter-Efron also argues that you must train your brain to respond automatically the way you want to respond in these moments of sudden emotion. That is the problem, he argues: Anger is an unconscious process and, in the few seconds you have, you can't use your conscious brain to overcome it. He recommends practicing, practicing, and practicing some techniques so your responses become automatic when certain moments arise. I am committed to deep breathing every day, and I do it at night with my children, too. I tell them (and granted this works better at ages older than toddler years), "Breathing helps us fall asleep, and it helps us stay calm so we can think about problems instead of getting angry." It's a powerful message to send to your children.

Identify Your Emotions in the Moment

The best advice I got for dealing with anger came from Dr. Tsabary in her book *The Awakened Family*. Dr. Tsabary's advice is to ask yourself, when you find yourself irritated, what you are feeling. Merely by bringing your emotion into conscious consideration, you can deal with it more effectively. You can take the sting out of a powerful emotion in just seconds, so necessary to how you operate as a parent. Dr. Tsabary writes directly about this issue—of being the parent you want to be versus reacting blindly. I can't recommend her work enough on this issue. It may also help a parent work through other issues of anxiety or worry. It's worth it to read the whole book on your own. It will help throughout all of parenthood.

Dr. Tsabary's main message is for parents to bring their emotion into conscious consideration. I have found, ever since I first performed this, that I become almost completely calm as a parent most of the time. When I notice irritation arising in me, I ask, "What am I feeling?" I can almost always make a much better decision. It also only takes seconds and identifying the emotion almost always calms the emotion down. The underlying feeling is often unrelated to the situation. The very first time I used it was when my son went to attack my daughter. I went to yell at him, a form of lashing out—not how I want to be as a parent—but I asked myself what I was feeling. It was this, "A fight would not break out like this in a school. I am failing as a homeschool mom." This thought of mine is untrue. I had a glorified, false vision of how preschools typically run. But by identifying my emotion, I was able to deal with it better. In this case, I said "Not today" to mom guilt, and I went on to handle the situation like a pro.

Dr. Tsabary clarifies the difference between a "feeling" and an "emotion." A feeling is something you feel. It's something to sit with, even if painful. An emotion, "motion," drives you to act. It's the emotions that need to be dealt with. Bringing them into conscious consideration tames them and turns them into feelings. Along these lines, it is my belief, shared by many experts, that anger is not something for you to vent, but something for you to contain, then process internally. As a responsible adult, a skill set to master is the art of self-soothing when these powerful emotions arise.

Dr. Gordon, who wrote *Parent Effectiveness Training*, advocates using "I" statements when negotiating with others, but he makes an exception for anger. He says that saying "I feel angry" always comes across as "You are making me angry," in other words, as being accusatory. Dr. Gordon says another feeling altogether usually lies under anger. He gives the example of a child coming home late. A parent might get angry with the child, but the underlying feeling is really one of worry. Calming your emotion down and getting to that underlying feeling is powerful. "I was so worried about you" is more effective to help resolve the situation in the future than anger. I find as I get experience with "I" statements, I can easily tell when an "I" statement is done out of a genuine and empathetic attempt to heal the conflict or if I am just lashing out. "I am really annoyed right now" is usually just exasperation and not helpful to the child. If making the statement "I am really annoyed right now" helps you calm down, so be it, if it prevents any other more harmful action.

In *Healing the Angry Brain*, Potter-Efron recommends being in touch with your emotions and cues to recognize early signs of anger coming on. Do your hands get cold? Do you start to tap your foot? I try to notice these signs, and I also try to notice common triggers that can start to raise my frustration level. A most common trigger for me is when I feel like I can take some "me" time, but then one of my children has a problem. When my child comes whining, "Help me, Help me," or when a fight breaks out, I can think to myself, "This is annoying, but I am annoyed because I wanted some me time." Do I want to become irritated and irate with my children just because I wanted to do some self-care for a little bit? The answer is no. I am able to flow better. I put down what I am doing, deal with the situation, and come back when I get the chance. Another trigger for me is when one kid is hitting another child. Being physically assaulted by one of your children is also a very common trigger. A crying child can be a trigger. A crying child can be a trigger for other children too, who then start acting up, compounding the situation further.

I put forth that healthy emotional management means being conscious of your own emotions, sharing non-threatening emotions with others by using effective "I" statements, but learning to contain and self-soothe any emotion that might cause you to lash out at or harm others or yourself. I now think of this as *emotional responsibility*.

Assume Success is Likely

I also learned from Dr. Tsabary something that can revolutionize nearly everything. If you don't already assume success is likely, next time your child has a meltdown, try this: Assume the child will likely cooperate. I find this works magic. As the child is in tears, I am not assuming failure is inevitable. I thus start thinking of clever ways to get them to cooperate. My calm seems to transfer to them. This buys me time more effectively than any other approach, including approaches directly meant to buy time. I had difficulty taking a "parent timeout." I found it was difficult to force myself to take time for the sake of taking time. But when I "assume success is likely," I naturally buy myself more time as I simply think through the problem. When the emotion you have is one of assured calm and not one of fear or pessimism, this disinfects many conflicts.

Similarly, assume abundance. Once, my infant son got his pants very dirty. I was at first upset, because I was having trouble keeping up with laundry at the time. Then I remembered that I had done laundry recently. It then became no big deal to simply change him. When I realized clean pants were in abundance, it helped me deal with the situation calmly. I have been in situations where abundance was quite available, but the parent might assume it was not. For instance, a child might be doing a project with a piece of paper but makes a mistake. Paper is usually very abundant and inexpensive. It should not be a big deal to get a new piece of paper, but I have seen parents yell at or correct a child or make the child reuse the paper with the mistake on it.

Even if material objects are not in abundance, if you assume that some solution somewhere is likely possible—that clever solutions are in abundance—it can change your attitude.

Describe the Situation

I find in a situation where I am only moderately upset, and I don't know what to do yet, I am benefited if I just start observing and describing the situation. One time, my son threw a cup of milk (with a lid). I was fairly upset, and by chance I just started thinking aloud, describing the situation, "I see a cup of milk on the floor." To my surprise, my son, then just a toddler, went and picked up the cup! Problem solved! One way I sometimes think about it is as an OODA loop. USAF Colonel John Boyd, a fighter pilot, developed the OODA loop. It stands for "Observe, Orient, Decide, Act." Being a parent and being a fighter pilot have their similarities.

Mom / Dad Timeout

Several books stress taking a parent timeout—that timeouts are best used by parents, not inflicted on children. I often couldn't use timeouts, a cooling period, for myself, because I couldn't leave a situation. It did work occasionally though. I used them when I was a new mom especially and I didn't know how to handle situations. I would occasionally just sit in a separate room, letting happen whatever would happen, as I tried to make sense of what was going on.

One time, I overheard my husband gasp in shock because our son, 4, had sprayed water all over the kitchen. I had just shown my son how to use the extendable faucet to clean, and I knew what had happened. I had gone to the other room to do my hair. In that time, I had time to think. This amount of time, which I was given as a gift by grace of doing my hair, helped immensely. I brought out two towels and said we could clean it up. My son, upset, sniffled, "I was trying to make the kitchen beautiful." I believed him. He needed to be consoled, not punished. Being away from the situation allowed me to think about it. What a luxury that was! Any situation where you can get more time to respond is always a good thing.

As I gain experience, I can stay present in the moment better and think quicker, and I find I don't need a timeout as much. But when I need it, I *need* it.

Mom Brain / Dad Brain

Mom Brain is a thing. It can happen to mom or dad or anyone. I wondered what a counter to Mom Brain would be. My husband once put leftover food in a cupboard instead of the refrigerator and said, "Oh! Stupid Dad Brain." Dad Brain seems like the logical corollary, and one that is already used in our house.

Mom or Dad Brain is a result of not being able to accomplish a singular goal due to being derailed by children so often. You can see it in visible action sometimes. When I go to put away a sock, I might, on my way, see garbage. I then throw away the garbage, and I might forget about the sock. Or I go and get the sock, and then come out, and see another sock, and put away that sock too, in two full trips. It goes on like this in infinite ways. A more logical approach would be to do a sweep of the room for all socks and do them at once—and not to get derailed by the garbage. But, after getting derailed like this with children over and over, sometimes the pattern gets etched in one's brain as a hard and unhappy habit.

Here is how I would describe this problem using my own trying times as a resource. I make no promises about the rightness or wrongness of my thoughts. I am simply describing what Mom Brain, which leads to Mom Burnout, can be like:

I woke up one Saturday morning and just started doing things. Dishes, laundry, organizing, responding to children, and in a way that was totally haphazard. My husband said in near bewilderment, "What are we doing? It feels like we have no … no plan." I had a really bad case of Mom Brain that day. Yes, no plan whatsoever. It can be maddening. You're just doing. Someone who was visiting asked me once, "What is your plan for today?" As I sat at the table, still not dressed for the day, having served everyone breakfast, staring down yet more diaper changes and requests for juice, the question annoyed me greatly. *Plan*? I don't plan anything. That is a luxury that people with free time have. My plan is to take care of three children. Help would be appreciated!

I told my husband once of a woman who divorced her husband when they had an infant, and the trigger for her was when she handed the baby to him and he asked for a washcloth. To my husband's enormous credit, he asked why this would trigger her. I explained that when you are a sole caregiver of a baby, you have to do everything. If you settle in to feed them, and then realize you forgot a washcloth, you have to get up to get it. No one is around to help you. These things just continue to add up. When you finally get a break—when you finally get a gasp of air—and the person who relieves you asks you for *one more thing*, it can be infuriating. Having to respond to each child, having to remember where they are in their growth, having to keep the house clean, putting away the toys that constantly seem to be out, not having a place to make a sandwich because the counters are so cluttered, can be more than crazy making.

It used to upset me greatly when visitors to our house would leave things "for when they come back." Why? Because it was one more thing. When you are a sole caregiver to children, especially multiple children, a package delivered at the front door can be like a tornado hit—because you have to leave a child who might be crying, because you might have been in the middle of doing a naptime routine, because another child is excited about the package, because you might not be dressed, because getting around if you are pregnant is hard. When I have to take care of three children all day, clean, get food, plan lessons, deal with whining, deal with them grabbing me, and not able to walk around, because they block me or beg me for attention so much, I would describe the feeling like Nik Wallenda as he walked on a tight rope across the Grand Canyon. Demanding, whining children who climb all over you feels like wind on your face and other elements as you try to accomplish some kind of goal, like making food, which feels like walking on a tight rope.

This type of thing can be the source of jokes, and this is one healthy way to cope with it, but I am not exaggerating when I say some of this can lead to serious mental illness. I think everyone probably has some breaking point, where trying to juggle everything becomes overwhelming. For some people, it might be after only one child. Others might be able to handle six or more. It's different for everyone, and some might break, then bounce back, then break again. I will never judge anyone for where their breaking point is, recognizing it is different for everyone.

I could tell that this Mom Brain was causing my brain to atrophy. Dealing with children can be constant, from early in the morning until late in the evening, not allowing for any space in which to think. One thing I did during some of the worst bouts of it was to focus on accomplishing one small goal if I could. For me, when my daughter would take her time getting ready in the morning, I would clean up her room. Then, when I came into her room later in the day, I could rest my eyes on a clean room and instead of being one more thing that was irritating; it was one little thing that uplifted me a little bit. Practicing deep breathing in moments where you are just sitting with a child can be soothing—and an act of accomplishment.

The remaining sections in this chapter are meant to help relieve and prevent Mom and Dad Burnout.

Refill Your Cup

There have been times when I was so behind and felt like I was drowning that even putting the effort to get outside help (babysitter or other sources) was overwhelming. Once I had a terrible day, mostly from dealing with toddler meltdowns in the late twos, and I really wanted a babysitter. But our recent babysitter didn't work out. I had to go back to the interview process to get one, on top of many other more pressing things. I knew it would take several days, if not weeks, just to get help, and I needed help right then.

When you are so in over your head like this, it is difficult to hear someone say, "Woah, you really need to get some help. Hire a babysitter." This is the equivalent of "Whoa, it looks like you're drowning out there. Maybe you could call the Coast Guard." I write about things like this so that maybe others will know what *not* to say to someone in over their head and so that I will remember in the future when someone else is going through it what it felt like, something people are so quick to forget. Never, *ever*, will you find me saying, "You'll miss those night feedings, dearie; you will, really!" I will accept the popular bromide told mothers, "The dishes can wait," if you tack on at the end, "for someone else to do them."

What was so refreshing to me was when someone would step in and do something to relieve the work load. This person was almost always my husband. Late at night, when I've been at it all day, I often didn't have it in me to try to brush my kid's teeth. While I sat, totally burned out, swearing off brushing their teeth ever again, resigning myself to many kid cavities, my husband would step in and do it. This was a major soul lifter. It was one *less* thing. And this was often all it took to revitalize me. It reaffirmed my commitment to quality parenting. I would compare the one more thing and one less thing to a clean house. If a house is clean, and you see one thing laying out, you probably clean it up. If the house is a mess, and one more thing gets left out, it piles up. You stop tending to it. As things get out of control, they continue to spin out of control. But if the process is reversed, and things start getting cleaned, it becomes more and more of an incentive to clean up. Doing one small thing for yourself (something other than picking up socks!) or having someone else do one small thing for you can turn everything around.

Thought needs to be put behind how you might get extra support to refill your cup. My husband's and my first approach to this was that we would switch off watching the kids as we both took personal time. If this works for you, I don't mean to tell you not to do this, but we found it did not work well. Let's say my husband left on a Saturday. This means after a long week of being with the kids, I am again at it on a day when I normally would have extra help. The only way I could get my break was to double up on a day that I otherwise got some break. And when my husband was there, the division of labor went into effect. It is *more* than doubly easy to take care of children when two adults are there, because you can divide up tasks so much better. Not having him around on a weekend was more than doubly hard. The fact was that both my husband and I were burned out at times and trying to be each other's support wasn't working. Being together was more fulfilling than being separate. At best, we could trade off for a half hour or a few hours at a time so the other could get a nap. Otherwise, finding external support was necessary.

Getting a steady babysitter worked better for us. It took me a while to find a babysitter situation that worked well, but here are a few principles I found to go about this process.

First, if you find a babysitter or nanny that you are paying a decent wage, expect service in return. When I was young, I used to babysit for neighbors. I was paid $2 per hour and I really did just sit with children. If you are paying someone $13/hour, expect that they are working the whole or most of the time. Sure, dealing with children might consume their entire shift. However, at down times, they can be working for you, not doing homework or texting. Having someone not just watch your kids, but also clean up a little around the house feels almost like magic if you've never experienced it. Interview a few people. Don't give anyone a job at the interview. I liked babysitters who said, "I am here for you. I want to relieve your burden." Issues of availability and expectations can cause the process to fail and are best ironed out perhaps even before the interview. Don't make any long-term commitments until you've tried them as a babysitter once or twice. I tend to give babysitters two chances at watching my kids, because I assume the first visit might have been overwhelming for them and that they need my input to make it a success. Some babysitters do better with a written list of how to do things and what your expectations are, so I make one no matter what and keep it out every time they are there. When I find a babysitter I like, I pay them well by checking standard rates for the area. Also, I give them a promise to keep up with those standard rates. I found it's best to have two or three sitters so that one babysitter doesn't feel pressured to be there for you always. Having help after the birth of a baby is ideal. If you have multiple children and two of them are under the age of 3, I recommend that you arrange help of some sort at least once per week. Enrolling your children in a class can also provide relief.

A problem arises in that you are most likely to ask for help from someone when you are dealing with your children during a difficult time, as when they are in an irritable period. My experience is other people sometimes claim that there is something wrong with the child and seek to find if the child is sick or needs a nap, when the child is simply in a natural and now documented phase of development. It is also difficult if you have adopted a non-punitive approach to parenting, and you have to ask a person not to use punitive means, which for many people is the only method they know to control the behavior. To help with this, on my website at TheObservantMom.com, I have a section on Cognitive Growth Spurts that offers free printouts that you can print and distribute to family, friends, and caregivers. For every age group for which I have information, I will maintain a PDF that will explain what cognitive growth spurts are, present a summary chart, and give highlights for each milestone. These milestones are an expanding, growing body of work so updates happen continuously. I hope to spread awareness and acceptance of cognitive growth spurts, and I invite you to join in this effort.

Mom Caves and Man Caves (Physical Boundaries)

There are times when I really needed a break to focus and think. I found if I was out in a communal area of the house, it was too enticing for any family member to come "connect" with me. I got a simple desk in my bedroom to go to when I needed to do something. It was my beloved Mom Cave or as I sometimes call it my "Command and Control Center." It is entirely respectful. It's a very real physical boundary—a closed door—letting others know what you need at that time. It's a lot better than being out, trying to be accommodating, when you really aren't in the mood, which possibly results in your getting exasperated and irritated. I admit that it seemed to be an initial shock to the whole family that mom would be in a separate room, something of which needed a bit of work for others to accept but which was worth it.

This work as a parent is difficult, important, and requires an investment. The work should be dignified as such, with a proper space and time to work. Proper parenting requires time to sit down and reflect on how to approach children. Respect the work that the primary caregiver does with a spot that they can retreat to where they can write down their observations, think of activities, ask advice, read, or do whatever it is they need to do in peace.

Many other such physical boundaries helped as well. I was reluctant for the longest time to put any infant child in a sectioned off area, for instance, a Pack N' Play. I valued my children's ability to roam and do what they wanted as they explored, and so I resisted doing this. I found, however, that it could be overwhelming to try to watch an infant child when you have older children in the house. I especially became overwhelmed after my third child was born. It was a constant rush to meet their demands, and as I rushed to get things done, my infant would find, for instance, dried up Play-Doh underneath the couch and munch on it. I finally put up a Pack N' Play. It really improved the situation. I found I didn't even use it often. I would put my infant in for 5 or 10 minutes, but often that was all I needed to deal with a situation or clean up a mess. And when I got him back out, I felt authentically ready to connect.

Put the Brakes On

When I found myself in over my head, I often took it as a time to put the brakes on. I would go through toys or clothes and get rid of what we didn't really need. I found my clarity improved greatly about what could go or not when I was, well, over it. Stuffed animals (which are often bulky) can go usually, beyond a few favorites (unless, of course, you find high value in them for any reason whatsoever), having four or five different rattles is usually unnecessary, and I had to accept that some toys were past their educational value, even if I previously saw them as being very beneficial.

I also saw these moments as a time to invest in some clean up or other discipline skills. If we were doing academic lessons hard, but the house was disorganized or cluttered, I would stop with formal academic lessons and focus on lessons about cleaning up the toy room or putting drinking cups back on the counter, and so on.

Quit

I found that much of this advice for staying patient worked, and well. I could stay present even in moments of emotional outburst. There were times, however, when I just had to *quit*. When my daughter was in Toddler Milestone 11 (2 years, 10 months) late at night one night, I just could not deal with her constant requests for attention. I left her in her room, went to our bedroom, and put a blanket over my head. I let my husband go in and deal with her. That's how it goes sometimes.

I once was in over my head trying to get to soccer practice (for my son, five years old at the time, though the whole family, toddler included, was affected and a factor). I could not manage to get all the stuff together to get out in time, despite my best efforts. I tried all the clever techniques I could think of to get my son motivated to go, as he was often reluctant. After several rounds of this, for one practice, I realized I had gotten what I thought was everything together—except I had forgotten to gather up his shin guards and I just didn't know where they were. My son was also reluctant to go; I was carrying around a fussy infant; and I had just spilled milk all over myself. That was it! I quit! We just did not go to soccer practice. I had the luxury of again hiding myself under a blanket. This eventually turned into a great positive for us. It very clearly communicated that I was at my breaking point. It communicated my need for help in this area to my husband. I verbally communicated to my son as gently as possible that it was his choice to continue to go to soccer or not. Not going, I think, may have shown him that I was not going to drag him. He had a choice: either get ready promptly and go or we're not doing this anymore. We also worked through some other issues that he had, but at the very next soccer event, my son got ready promptly and announced his excitement for soccer!

You don't have to slog along at all times, especially if you feel you are fighting others for their own benefit. Quitting something can be healthy. You have a right to invest in things that bring you and/or your family value and divest yourself of things that don't.

Repair Attempts

The fact is you will likely lose control sometimes. Every parenting book I have ever read says this will happen. Perfection is not the goal. When you do mess up, forgive yourself, apologize to anyone you hurt, and recognize that it was temporary. I see these as great learning opportunities for children. You can sincerely apologize to them and tell them that what you did was wrong, modeling for them what an authentic apology from an authentic grownup looks like. I believe in showing children clear opposite ways of doing things as a wonderful way to learn. In this way, when you mess up but then apologize, you have shown them both the right and wrong way of doing things. I don't recommend losing it on purpose for this reason, but when it happens, it can be worked into a positive. Wake up the next day remembering that you have it in you to be awesome.

It is so important to talk to your spouse or other caregivers about this issue. It is important to recognize that other people have different breaking points or triggers than you do and that, over the course of parenting, you both will hit a breaking point. I love the idea of using a "safe word." If one spouse is overwhelmed, they can use it, and leave the situation if need be and if at all possible. Recognize your significant other has grumpy days and breaking points too.

Professional Help

If you are still struggling with anxiety or anger, there may be an underlying problem. I'd like to recommend *The Body Keeps Score* by Dr. Bessel van der Kolk. In this book, Dr. van der Kolk tells the story of his career in healing patients with trauma. He describes dealing with veterans, sexual assault survivors, people with developmental trauma (being abused or neglected as a child), and other difficult contexts. He provides so many examples of patients that he has treated, ranging from veterans who saw awful things in war to people whose parents "joked" about getting the wrong child that you may be able to see yourself in the examples he gives. In using those examples, you may have a better idea of what kind of therapy might work for you. His therapies often focus on more bodily therapies such as yoga, massage, and dance, but he discusses a wide range of therapies and when they might apply. He is a passionate advocate for treating unresolved trauma, which is the root of many physical and emotional problems. Even if you don't think you have much of a problem in the way of unresolved trauma, I think you may find that this book helps you up your game when it comes to staying patient, calm, and loving. Dr. van der Kolk's goal is to help people not simply not be angry, anxious, or depressed, but to "feel fully alive." I am moved by his book and recommend it to everyone.

Becoming a parent can be and is truly transformational. These skills make one a better parent and person.

Dealing with the Child's Emotions

The book *Liberated Parents, Liberated Children* by Adele Faber and Elaine Mazlish is a fantastic book and a must read for parents. Both authors are students of Dr. Ginott, the author of *Between Parent and Child*. This book profoundly changed the way I dealt with my children. The following sections offer a few of the book's main messages, how these helped our family, and how this philosophy—described as a "validating feelings" model—can be easily integrated into an observant parenting style.

I include this in my book on toddlers, because at 2 years, 1 month, big emotions start to surface. Knowing how to deal with them is vital.

Validate Feelings

The most powerful and intellectually riveting theme throughout *Liberated Parents, Liberated Children* is to validate a child's feelings.

Reading about validating feelings came just at the right time for me, when my oldest son (my first born) was 2 years and 1 month old. At this age, I found that big emotions verbally stated started to surface.

My first experience was during the summer in Florida, when it thunderstorms violently a lot. One day, thunder cracked. My son became visibly scared and even said, "John scared." I told him "It's thunder; it's nothing to be scared of." As I was saying it, I regretted the words coming out of my mouth and wanted to kick myself. Here I was reading all about validating children's feelings, meditating on the nuances of how this applies, and for this very simple emotion, I was telling him not to feel it, that he should feel what I wanted him to feel, i.e., I was externally manipulating him.

A few days later, suddenly and unexpectedly, thunder cracked. My son became visibly scared again and again said, "John scared!" This time I was prepared. Using descriptive language, I told him, "It's thunder," and then I validated his feelings the best way I knew how: I put my hand on his knee and said, "It's OK to be scared." For the next crack of thunder, he said, without even a hint of fear and with enthusiasm, "Thunder! John is scared of thunder!" He said this in the same way he might have said, "John is going to ride a train!"

I was truly stunned by this. He seemed as excited about identifying his emotion as he was when he first learned what a "ball" or the "moon" was. For the next several days, when thunder roared, he simply said, "John is scared of thunder," and kept doing what he was doing. Validating his feelings did not cause him to curl up into a ball—it empowered him.

From then on, he informed me of his feeling of being scared of many things. This included a dragon on a blanket, which I was then able to roll up for him. It also included telling me he was scared when another child was chasing him—but that time, he liked it. I could have kept telling him, "Don't be scared!" But how long would it take before he started to hide his feelings from me? Or for him to learn that his emotions weren't important? When he was older, on his own, with no pressure from us, when he was afraid of things, he would often say, "But I am going to be brave!" Had I ordered him to not be scared, would he ever learn that bravery is not the *absence* of fear, but *confrontation* of fear?

Emotions act as important catalysts. Let's take the thunder example one step further. Imagine that humans did not live in houses. If so, thunder would be the first warning to go seek shelter from dangerous lightning, wind, and rain. If thunder cracked and an adult told a child to not be scared, the child's emotions would be scrambled in such a way to work against his own survival.

This has a practical application today. Think of the child whose parents tell him that he should override his feeling of not wanting to kiss a relative because being kissed is something the relative would like. Now consider the contradiction that will set in the child's mind when his parents tell him, "No one should touch you in a way you don't like," and, in fact, shortly thereafter, someone does force the child to be touched in a way he does not like. It is this very "something isn't right" feeling that can potentially save children's lives; let your children learn to trust it. All emotions, even the "bad" ones, have a purpose.

It is an enormous gift to children to identify, validate, and help your children understand their own emotions. Children are not lying when they say they are scared, upset, or cold. How comfortable children will become when they learn that their emotions are allowed to be felt, that what they are feeling is actually real—that they are heard and that it is OK! When emotions are allowed to be felt, you can then deal with them in appropriate ways.

What is being described here is empathy. There is much confusion about empathy. Empathy does not mean "help others." It also does not mean "agree with others." It simply means to turn a listening ear to children and to understand their feelings about something that is their own and is different from yours. Dr. Ginott says this should be done in a short way, "turn a paragraph into a sentence; a sentence into a word; a word into a gesture" (ch. 4).

Many say that this approach of validating feelings is the *emotional* approach and not validating feelings is the *rational* approach. I would like to submit an argument that validating emotions *is* the rational (observant) approach, and that it is not a matter of emotions versus reason, but some other continuum. After an explanation, I will make my case for which continuum.

Let's imagine the opposite of validating feelings using two adults. Imagine a wife who said she was cold in their house, and the husband says, "Don't be silly, it's hot in here." Any person somewhat familiar with married life can tell you how this response from the husband might make the wife feel and even react. She would be upset, possibly angered. Or, if she does slink away and get a blanket or sweater, resentment will build.

Would you consider the husband's response to be "rational"? Was his interpretation of how the temperature felt on his skin unequivocally correct? Was he the much smarter and more rational person and, thus, able to dictate the temperature of the house? Quite the contrary, in this story, the husband was insensitive, arrogant, and borderline-abusive. If the husband had at least recognized that his wife was cold, i.e., had empathy, would the result be more *loving* or less?

Let's look further at what is meant by this "rational" model as applied to parenting. I'd like to use two examples.

First example: A family is in the car and a young boy wants to get home right away, because he is hungry or has to use the bathroom and keeps complaining and complaining. The parent tells the child that they are stuck in traffic and can't get home until they get home; he then orders the boy to stop complaining. After all, those are the *facts* of the matter.

Second example: A family is about to leave an amusement park. A child wants to go on one more ride. The parent explains to the child that it is late, that they have a long drive, and they must go. The child then has a tantrum, and the parents yell at the child, "We'll just wait until you are done!"

Situations like this play out way more than thousands of times a day, every single day. Here are some alternative solutions where emotions are validated.

It is true in the first example that the family is stuck in traffic. That is a fact and contributes to why this model is considered "rational." It is acceptable to give this fact to the child, stating it once. What is not acceptable is telling the child to stop complaining about it, i.e., how to feel and how to react. Consider how the following solutions might play out. You might say to the child, "Oh Honey, I know you are so hungry," or describe how you are going as fast as you can to get home, because you understand his hunger, or indulge the fantasy of getting home by wishing for a flying car that could get out of traffic.

In the case of the family leaving the amusement park, where the child wants to stay, and the adults want to go, imagine it is two adults leaving the amusement park. One wants to stay, and another wants to go. One argues that it is getting late and another argues that they could squeeze in one more ride. Is the adult who wants to go more rational—or do they just have a different preference? Could the two negotiate or see each other's viewpoints?

This situation happened to us. My son, who was three years old at the time, wanted to go on a ride, but we couldn't, as it was late. I tried a few tactics, but when I finally asked if he wanted to talk about the ride, he sniffled, "Yes." The tears started to stop. I then held him, described the ride in thorough detail to him and reminisced on how much fun it was. As I did this, we walked peacefully to our car. After we started driving, he was asleep quickly. How long and how unsettling would it have been to argue with a small child about the rightness of getting to the car? Instead, I saw his viewpoint and indulged his fantasy, and the result was peace.

This is my argument: The rational model is the one where feelings are validated, that feelings are what they are, and that they must be dealt with, therefore, as immutable facts of reality. That is what rationality is—accepting that reality is what it is, that A is A (The Law of Identity). If you've told someone who says they are cold ("A") that they are hot ("B"), you have just invalidated their feelings *and* the Law of Identity. Telling a person that they are hot when they are cold doesn't alter the fact that they are cold. Feelings exist. They are there. In this case, it is the feelings that are the facts.

When you don't deal with things as they are, the result is abuse, poverty, and stagnation. If a chemist treated sulfuric acid ("A") as water ("B"), and drank it, the result is damage to the body. But when reason is applied correctly, the result is prosperity. In the hard sciences, it has brought humankind medical technology, computers, cars—the list goes on. Similarly, when you treat *emotions* as invalid, when you don't treat emotional facts as true, the result is unhappiness, anger, and hatred. But when you apply reason, the Law of Identity, to emotions, the result is love. *Love*, not simply "emotions," but as "reason applied to emotions" is the right description of this parenting style. Parents who use this model tend to have very calm, peaceful, loving homes. And embracing unhappy emotions is what leads to happy ones. It is thus that one side of the continuum of parenting styles, I propose, is love, defined as reason (acceptance) applied to emotion.

What has been described previously as the "rational" approach is not one of rationality, but of a parent being assumed to be older and thus more knowledgeable and able to dictate their "facts" (their judgment of a situation) to children. They are given the power to make decisions on behalf of the child, without the child's input. This isn't rationality. This is authoritarianism. Thus, the other side of the continuum, I propose, is authoritarianism.

This issue is not emotion versus reason, but of love versus authoritarianism. This issue is one of being an attentive, listening, responsive parent or a calloused, insensitive, arrogant one. Invalidating emotions is not rational. It is abusive.

I let my children feel what they feel. In the example of a husband arguing with a wife over the temperature of the house, this happens often with children. Parents insist a child needs a jacket when the child does not want one. I let my children have the choice of what they want. I have a formal lesson in the toddler years where I take the children outside in the moderate cold, and I say, "This is cold." Then I put a jacket on them and say, "This keeps you warm." Children are not dumb; they will seek comfort when they want it. I find my children are often more insistent than I am on wearing proper protective outer wear.

The title of my blog is "The Observant Mom," because I have found that observation is the central skill for quality parenting. An observant parent, from the day a child is born, looks for signs and cues as to what is happening with the child, such as sleepy signs and hunger signs when the child is an infant. From reading about validating children's emotions from these enlightened authors, let emotions be another sign to look for as you observe your children. Children's emotions should be as glaringly obvious to a parent as a bruise on their arm or the words coming out of their mouths and should be considered as one makes parenting decisions.

Soothe Upset Children Before All Else

Another most important point that I gleaned from *Liberated Parents, Liberated Children* was that emotions need to be dealt with first. While children are upset, absolutely no lectures or lessons can be given. If children are upset, the goal is always to soothe them first.

This idea confused me at first, but the notion became clear when I saw it in action with my son. My son had thrown all the magnets off our refrigerator. We asked him to clean them up. He didn't. Instead he got upset, started crying, and asked for food. I think many people would have seen giving him the food as "rewarding bad behavior." After not getting anywhere with picking up the magnets, I told my husband I'd like to try something. I gave my son some food to eat. He instantly calmed down. Immediately after eating, he cleaned up the magnets! Both my husband and I were astonished.

Imagine the last time you were in pain or simply frustrated. Let's say you burned dinner. If your spouse said to you, "That's what you get when you take your eye off the frying pan!" how would you react? You might be hurt and defensive. Or if you just had a heart attack, would the time you were in writhing pain be the appropriate time to be lectured about your diet? The worst case I have ever heard of concerned when a teenage girl got pregnant. During delivery, her mother refused to let her have any pain relief and screamed at her daughter that this is what she got for having premarital sex. What do you think of this mother, who dished out life lessons while her daughter was in unbearable pain—that she was abusive? (Nurses eventually had this mother removed from the hospital room.) This is what lectures while a child is in pain look and feel like.

Emotions come first. There can be no reasoning, lecturing, lessons given, or orders followed while children are upset. A related pearl of wisdom from Dr. Ginott: "only after a child feels right can he think right." I have implemented this practically by never, ever, trying to give a lesson, lecture, or otherwise do anything with children while they are in pain—either physically because they hurt themselves or emotionally because they are upset. If a child is crying, my goal as a parent, always, is to calm them down. I see my main role as a parent as "Comforter-In-Chief."

As an example of how not to implement this is, for instance, if a child takes a tumble down the stairs and, while the child is crying, the parent lectures, "That's what you get when you play on the stairs!" Or after suffering some mean taunts at the hands of a friend, a child may be in tears and the parent lectures, "Sticks and stones may break your bones…" Instead, empathize when the child is in pain. After the pain is gone, then re-evaluate the situation to see what could have been done better. The child must be in a calm state of mind to do post analysis. My favorite way to describe this comes from Siegel and Bryson in *The Whole-Brain Child*, "It's as if you are a lifeguard who swims out, puts your arms around your child, and helps him to shore before telling him not to swim out so far next time" (ch. 2). This is why (non-sermonizing) family meetings, role modeling, and separate lessons work so well: you take the child away from an intense situation and explain ideal behavior to the child from within a calm situation.

Another thing that confused me is why asking direct questions of children—appealing more to their minds than their feelings—wasn't advised by most experts who deal with children. But when I saw this in action, it was easier to understand. How many parents will have this short conversation with their child today alone: "How was your day?" "Fine." And that's it. The parent can't get anything else out of the child. Imagine that a police investigator sits you down in a bare room, shines a light on you, and demands you answer some tricky questions right then and there, all dealing with your past actions and emotions. You might shut down a bit? Now how about if a friend handed you a coffee, sat down next to you, didn't start in on who-what-when-why-where questions right away, but with some small talk, and slowly warmed up to the bigger questions? When I realized this, I realized why direct questions often don't get very far with children.

For this reason, I am opposed to asking children (toddlers especially) to "use their words." While children are upset or in pain, the adult is placing more demands on them to "use their words"—to perform what can be an enormous task of introspection. If children are in a clear state of mind, have developed a robust vocabulary, and feel safe in communicating with parents, they *will* "use their words," on *their* initiative and out of their own self-interest. Until then, the adult needs to help them untangle what they are going through emotionally. For children, learning how to verbalize their emotions through words instead of aggression is a long, tumultuous process that you can expect to deal with throughout the toddler and preschool years.

If, when your children are upset, they insult themselves, validate the feeling but never the insult, a recommendation from *Between Parent and Child*. They may say, "I am so stupid; I can't pass a spelling test." The response is, "You are frustrated that you didn't do well on the spelling test." This one is hard to do. My son once drew something, decided it was wrong, and crumpled it up. It is very easy to say "Honey! Why did you do that!? I thought it was lovely!" This just makes things worse. Instead, simply, "You didn't like what you drew?" Then, watch as they themselves work diligently towards fixing what they saw as a mistake. Don't get in the way of self-improvement!

To be sure, it is only the "bad" emotions that you must deal with. Good emotions are easy— rejoice in your child's happiness! I have found the bad emotions are like weeds in your yard. They may be undesirable, but if not managed, they overwhelm everyone. When parents ignore their child's negative emotions, perhaps even telling them "stop sulking" or ordering them to "have a good attitude," the result is the bad emotions grow wild and untamed and hang over everyone's head like a dark cloud.

I have embraced that my children will be upset many times in their life. It is something to empathize with, try to soothe, and sometimes even just let fizzle out. It is not something to "correct." It is simply part of humanity, and as a parent, you will deal with it from meltdowns from toddlers to grumpiness from teenagers. No one is always happy or never complains. When my children are having a meltdown, I sometimes remind myself that the goal isn't entirely to end the meltdown. Sometimes it is to just sit with them through their pain.

Many parents report how their children are well-behaved at school but a big ball of emotions at home, and they wonder what they are doing wrong. This happens because a child's parents are his or her safe spot. I consider it to be an *honor* that my children come to *me* with their big emotions. It is a privilege to be the person that deals with this side of them.

Descriptive Praise

Another powerful message from the authors is to use "descriptive language" instead of "value judgments," when praising a child. When I first read this advice, I thought it meant to never coach, explain, or comment on a child's work at all—just being completely silent or at the very least, completely impartial. But that is not what the authors mean.

Let me start with praise. It's a lot more fun! Instead of being generic or over-the-top with praise, the authors instead advocate to be very specific and descriptive in how you praise. The classic example is when a child brings you a drawing. Some typical reactions are to give generic praise such as "What a nice painting!" or to give global praise such as "You are the best artist ever!" Instead, take an interest in the work and describe it. For a toddler you might say, "I see how you chose green to draw this long line and red to color this curvy line." Certainly, this approach is better than giving a perfunctory, "Great job, kid," or worse, insulting the work. If you give a description of the work, you are taking an interest in what they did, and having others take an interest in one's work is what every creator of any age wants.

Authors Faber and Mazlish in *How to Talk so Kids Will Listen* recommend praising with just one word if possible. If the child cleans up her room, you can say, "That's what I call cleanliness!" This gives the child a "verbal snapshot" of him or herself. Dr. Ginott in *Between Parent and Child* says to give the description of what the child did, but not the natural conclusion. An example given is a child who moves some furniture. The adult may say, "It was very hard to move that bench." The child then says, "Yes! I am very strong!" The child concludes this on their own. I personally like to give the evidence and conclusion when children are young. This is a matter of vocabulary building. A toddler may have never heard the word "strong." When they push a wagon that was moderately heavy, you can say, "It was hard to push that wagon. You are strong!" Now they might know the word.

Some people say they don't praise their children because it's "their" judgment of the work and not the child's own assessment. It may be true that one should learn to judge their own work and stand by it (and I think this comes more from loving yourself, knowing you are never "bad" but just in error, which is greatly developed simply from having loving parents), but throughout all of life, one has to sell their work and themselves to *others*. To get a job, you must convince an employer to hire you. To own a business, you need to convince customers to buy your product. When dating, others' opinions of you clearly matter. Knowing where you stand with others and having others reflect back to you what they see as good in you is healthy and vital. I can tell you that the entire reason I wrote this book and wrote it in the way that I have is because others told me they saw value in my parenting ideas and the research I had done. This feedback allowed me to direct my investment into something that might be helpful to people. Having feedback from others about what they see as good in you is simply necessary, no matter what age you are.

Maybe it would help to think of this not as giving praise but as giving compliments. Adults freely give compliments to each other often. My husband once bought fish at a seafood counter and noticed the woman working, on her first try, got the weight exactly right. He complimented her on this, and it clearly brightened her day. I don't see why we shouldn't go around complimenting each other freely and generously with accurate observations and genuine admiration. Children need compliments too and, in fact, more. "For children to develop a worthwhile sense of themselves, they need to hear and overhear mostly positive remarks about themselves" (Ginott, Ginott and Goddard, ch. 2).

It has often been said to "praise effort not accomplishments." This advice gets so confused. The very psychologist who advanced this notion, Carol Dweck, has come out against giving the much-maligned "participation trophies" (Merryman). (Dweck's argument is that if such an award is to be given, it should be given about something specific, e.g., great spirit.)

I can offer some clarity on the issue with examples of when I have found praising effort to be helpful and when unhelpful. When my son was learning how to ride a bike (at three years old, using a balance bike at first), I found at first that the experience was a bit scary and overwhelming. What worked well was to praise him for "practicing," i.e., effort. I knew, as we were out on the sidewalk, I could have said, "If you keep trying, you'll get it!" This would have backfired, because it is an insult. It would have emphasized that he has *not* got it yet, that he is in an inferior state. You can't emphasize accomplishment when the child is still practicing. Instead, I praised him for practicing, and this infused him with confidence as he was trying. The first day he tried, even though did not ride a bike, he came home to tell his dad, "I did it! I did it!" And he did—he hadn't learned to ride a bike yet, but getting up on that big, scary bike was an accomplishment. The very next day he got it: he was up and riding a bike! And every time he is out, he says, "Mommy! I'm practicing!" What worked about this is that as he was trying, in the moment, I was praising effort—I praised what I saw. We were still in the middle of practice, and there would be future practice the next day.

Now consider a "participation trophy." It is given after the season is done. It can do no good: No further improvement is possible. Praising effort is patronizing at that point.

I take issue also with the idea of never praising accomplishment, or, at least, only ever praising effort. My son, when he was a toddler, often put together wooden train tracks, and he made different configurations every time he did it. When he would make a train track and come up to me, excitedly, I described what I saw: I see a bridge here, and a loop, and it's very windy through here. I noticed it and I noticed the details, and I especially noted when he did something impressive. I didn't just say, "Wow! Great! You were so focused and worked hard on this!" In my estimation, as I am describing what I see in front of me, he knows that it took a brush of creativity to put the train track around a certain obstacle, which I noticed. If I only ever "praised effort," I would be left tongue tied, unable to make appreciative statements about what I saw.

This is why I favor *descriptive praise*. I praise what I see, based on my genuine admiration. Children crave this. It is vital that you do it as a parent. I praise effort, accomplishment, the details of a creative effort—whatever is before me. It is genuine, detailed, and so very observant. Note that by describing the work, you can and will likely make value judgments, such as "how pleasant!" or "how thoughtful!" The authors even say praise is fine; it just needs to be done better. In *Liberated Parents, Liberated Children*, the authors, quoting Dr. Ginott, their mentor, "[T]elling a child he's 'good' is [not] necessarily bad; it's just not good enough" (58). If you are worried that your praise will be evaluative, it may help to think of it as you giving your personal feelings about the work as opposed to being a person who is judging them. The following statements give a person feeling: "I am appreciative that you cleaned up your toys." "I really like the detail on this clay sculpture that you made." You give "I" statements instead of "You" statements.

This approach to praise, by being highly descriptive and more personal than judgmental, is powerful. It infuses the child with actual self-confidence. He isn't just told he is good but *why* he is good. He is not just a "good boy," he is a boy capable of making a good drawing or fixing the sink or telling the truth or any number of things. You are helping raise the child's awareness of who he is as an individual, provided you give genuine admiration for what the child does. You are helping him to see what his strengths are. This can go a long way towards many things, not the least of which is choosing a future career path. And there is nothing quite like observing, for yourself, your own strengths that gives a person actual self-confidence. If parents praised a child's genuine traits, it makes a world of difference. You are a "light reflector" to your child, helping what is best in them flourish. This latter approach to praise is child-centered. It absolutely is part of observing your child.

On the subject of reason versus emotion, let me say that this approach of using descriptive language aligns perfectly with an observant (reason-based) approach. Reason is the process of using facts to reach a conclusion. When you give descriptive praise, you are pointing out some facts of what the child does and then coming to a conclusion (even if you don't state it). For instance, "You cleaned up your entire room." (The evidence) "You are very responsible!" (The conclusion) Or, "You have beautiful, shiny hair" (The evidence) "You are beautiful!" (The conclusion) Or, "You worked very hard at that painting." (The evidence) "You are very focused." (The conclusion) Descriptive praise *is* reason-based praise. Reason is description. That's what reason is: a total commitment to observing, understanding, and acting in accordance with the facts of reality. A quote from Ayn Rand that struck me when I read it is, "A physical science would not permit itself (not yet, at least) to ignore or bypass the nature of its subject. Such an attempt would mean: a science of astronomy that gazed at the sky, but refused to study individual stars, planets, and satellites" (Rand 15). By nature, reason is not generic but very specific and detailed.

Now, moving on to insults. Don't use them—ever. Insults are not motivators. You cannot change someone by making them feel bad about themselves. It is not helpful; it is demoralizing. "Many parents label their children stupid, lazy, and a cheat, yet expect such labels to motivate them to change into bright, industrious, and honest people" (Ginott, Ginott and Goddard, ch. 4).

A similar approach of not insulting children appear in the books in the *Positive Discipline* book series by Nelsen et al. The authors argue that you cannot change a person by making them feel bad about themselves, such as with "blame, pain, or shame." This is why the authors are opposed to spankings or timeouts (punitive discipline) as a method of behavior modification. Let's also add insults, labels, and physical or emotional pain to the list of things that do not improve a person. This again does not mean turning a blind eye to problems. But, instead of insults, a child who struggles with something warrants training, coaching, teaching, and encouragement.

This extends to all areas of the child's life. What good does it do if children are struggling with spelling to tell them, "You have terrible spelling!"? Or if they are socially awkward around peers, what good does it do to say to a child, "You are such a *dork!*" Or even worse, why make fun of an overweight child as being "fat" or "chubby." Instead, give these children the tools they need for improvement.

Another closely related evil to insults is "roles." A role is an insult but worse because it has the unspoken implication "and you'll always be that way" attached at the end. An insult may be "You were clumsy," a role may be "Here is Susie, whom we have nicknamed Butterfingers." I am opposed to punishment, but I think insults and especially "roles" are much worse. Punishment in its weird way is growth mindset. It says, "You were wrong but through this punishment you can become right." I don't agree with this method, but a role says, "You're awful and you'll always be awful." It's terrible. It is plainly the worst thing that can be done to a child—and when looking at children who become violent as adults, we must not only look at if they were abandoned or physically abused but if they were emotionally abused in this way, as it is much worse. Instead, you as a parent may say, "I have confidence that in the future you can be careful when doing the dishes." The book *Positive Discipline: A – Z* describes the phrase, "Let's try again later" (Nelson, Lott and Glenn, "The 'Good Child'") as a magical phrase. I use it often as a parent, such as, "I can't let you have this toy if you are going to hit with it. Let's try using it again later." This phrase *is* magic. It says to a child, "You are doing something incorrectly or harmful for now. It is temporary. This is something you can work on to improve later."

Ultimately, the message contained in *Liberated Parents, Liberated Children*, and in this chapter, is that the tender creature that is your child, who is to become an adult, must be built with the utmost respect for who they are using genuine love, support, and encouragement. When I look at my children's faces, and think of this approach, I think of it as ultimate love. This approach completely rejects any insults or pain as supposed growth measures. Yet at the same time, the child's spirit is developed, piece by piece, through challenges that they work through on their own with but gentle guidance.

Being observant of your child's feelings fits in perfectly with an observant, rational approach to parenting. You simply take their emotional state into consideration when making decisions as you would the words coming out of their mouths or physical signs of health. It is easy enough and simple enough to notice and say, "I see you are sad," or "I see this makes you happy!" Ignoring or denying these emotions can only result in children who don't understand their own emotions, don't trust them, and becomes callous. Validating emotions is not at odds with a rational approach, or an observant approach, but is flawlessly in line.

Setting Healthy Boundaries with Your Toddler

It is important to know how to set your own boundaries with your toddler. By boundaries, I mean *your* boundaries. What actions do *you* find unacceptable to you and for what reasons as they relate to *you*? Everyone has some. Imagine it like a room in which you have put up a "don't go behind this line" rope to section off certain areas. Now think about how to enforce that effectively.

Recognize first that setting boundaries is for your sake—not the child's. Although setting healthy boundaries can model ideal behavior, it is not for the child's sake that you do it, such in the way that some say that the child "needs to learn to accept 'No' as an answer." There was a popular video that floated around on social media entitled "Is Your Child Getting Enough Vitamin N?" (Rosemond). "Vitamin N" is the word "No." This argument proposes that it is for the health of the child that the child hears the word "No," as if it's a vitamin that the child needs. The usual example for this argument is the child who wants a toy, and the parent says "No," and the child screams. It is taken as an important learning moment for the child to hear "No" in this instance. This is exactly what I am opposed to and exactly what I want to address.

I can agree that children "need" to and can and will eventually learn to respect others, but what your need is at the moment in setting your own boundary and what the child is capable of learning are on two separate timelines. As far as learning to hear "No," I find in the late fours, the child becomes extremely receptive to ideas of consent and this can easily be taught at that time. As far as learning to persist at a challenge without immediate gratification, this is developed through hands-on practice as they work towards bigger and bigger challenges. Their timeline is their developmental timeline, but your timeline for what you need is immediate. What you need in the moment is for the child not to get into the medicine or to stop being reckless or to get out of the store without unwanted items. These are separate things. You can get your needs satisfied while decoupling them from the development of the child.

In the example of the child at the store who wants a toy, my standard approach is to give the child an allowance of a small amount, perhaps $1 per week, and tell them they have their money and it's their choice to spend money on it or not. This approach works every time.

The child usually becomes calm and understanding and often surprise me with what they say or how well they understand the idea of money. And "saying 'no'" never works. The child becomes distraught, and no observation I have ever made has led me to believe that the child has learned a lesson. And let me ask you which of these is in better alignment with what children will face as adults—the one where children learn to "hear no" or the one where they are allowed to make a choice within the financial means that they have and live with the consequences? If a child is too young to understand money (you might try an allowance in the late twos or early threes), I might indulge their wish but put the toy back or try to distract them.

The issue here isn't one of indulging or not the child's every material wish. If I had to pick between living in a family in total material poverty, but who recognized that my needs and dreams were important, or a family with abundant material wealth but lectured me to "be grateful for the food and shelter you are provided and don't ask for any more," I would pick the former. Would you rather have a doctor who said, "No, I can't help you, and I am not interested in listening to your problems" or one who says, "Yes, I will work on finding a solution"? Or, if the doctor can't, then tells you with full sorrow that there is nothing more she can do? The issue here is *attitude*.

There is virtually no risk of a child growing up "without ever hearing no." My first child, as a toddler, once wanted me to take the steering wheel off the car and hand it to him. Life has many resource constraints, and you will have to say no to the child. And what is better: saying "no" with kindness and reason or saying "no" for no reason whatsoever? Imagine someone could provide something for you but didn't, so you would "learn a lesson." I have read many self-help books and one recurring theme is that, as children, the adults did not receive enough love and support. The issue is never that they "didn't have enough discipline" or "enough rules" or "enough boundaries" or "never heard no." The issue is that love is too scarce. And I also do not think love is "free." Love is something to practice routinely and must be actively cultivated. Acts of love within relationships require labor. They are far from free.

The child doesn't need to *hear* "no"; you need to learn to *say* "no." If you adopt the attitude that setting boundaries is for your sake, you teach the child, day in and day out, what firm but kind boundaries look like. It's real and it's authentic. You're getting your needs satisfied; they in time will learn to respect boundaries. Happily, they, modeling you, might learn how to set their own boundaries (say "no") with others.

I adopted an approach where I tried to say "yes" to my children as often as I could, while staying true to my own authentic feelings by saying "no" if I really didn't want to do something. The attitude that children can develop from this is great. I found my children did what I did, not what I said. By my understanding their need and working towards a solution, they then responded in kind. One time when my son was a toddler, he decided to serve people green beans. When people would ask for them, he would say, "Coming right up!" He adopted the very language that we had in which we tended to his needs. My children are often understanding of my mistakes and are respectful of my needs, which I credit with tending to their needs so fully for years. I am bursting with pride over my children's patience, kindness, and empathy.

Many books offer advice on how to set up healthy boundaries with children of all ages. I break this advice down into what works for toddlers. In the early toddler years, children don't have much reasoning capability. Getting them to respect you involves a lot of gentle hands-on methods, such as moving them. In the late twos, however, children show empathy, grow dramatically in reasoning capability, understand simple ideas of right and wrong, and actively try to understand the function of something. It is with these ages in mind that this chapter has been written. This approach, which relies mainly on offering the child information, is one that appeals to children's reason and growing sense of right and wrong and does not demand blind obedience. These methods take advantage of the fact that children, and humans in general (depending on their life experiences), naturally want to do what is right and have a deep inclination in them not to hurt people.

In understanding toddlers, however, one can understand that they still have a deep need to be taught right from wrong. Thus, the methods employed are ones that teach and instruct, usually without as much input from the child as you would elicit at older ages.

When you must make in-the-moment decisions as a parent, it helps sometimes to have short phrases in your mind ready to apply to a situation. I have two different such short phrases for the following tools. One I refer to as the two I's: "I" statements and Information. Another is "strong demonstrations and clear expectations." I found that having a short phrase in my head helped me think on the spot better. For instance, my son once kept running down a sidewalk at a place we went to routinely, while I had to carry his infant sister and a bag. Having the phrase, "clear expectations" in my brain, I had the idea to bring chalk and draw on the ground an "X" to get him to stop running and stand at that spot. It worked!

However you want to see it, these methods do not rely on pressuring the child (or sarcasm or invoking pity), but rather on raising the child's awareness to a problem or an ideal behavior. These methods can dominate the late twos and much of the threes and fours (with yet more tools being added in the threes and fours).

"I" Statements

In the late twos, "I" statements start to become effective. I use them at all times, even if they don't "work," because I think they are the proper way to set my own personal boundaries with children or adults. However, in the late twos, children start to respond to them. "I" statements are great because they set your personal boundaries without taking away any of the fun that implementing an overarching rule might risk doing.

As an example, once my toddler son was jumping all over me. I didn't like it. I simply said, "It hurts me when you jump on me." Well, his dad didn't mind at all. He went over and jumped on his dad, much to both of their delight. Had I said "No jumping!" I would have squashed this benevolent fun.

There is an art to effective "I" statements. I learned about them from Dr. Gordon's, *Parent Effectiveness Training*, which I think is an absolute must read for parents at the latest by the time children are five, preferably by the time they are two and a half. First, Dr. Gordon describes when to use them. It has to be decided first if the problem is your problem or the child's problem. If they have the problem, you employ active listening. (I describe empathy and active listening in my chapter on children's emotions.) If *you* have a problem, you state it with an "I" statement. He asks readers to imagine if a guest in your house had their feet on furniture and you didn't like it. Would you say, "Don't put your feet on the couch!" or "You are being disrespectful!" No, you would say something like, "I hate to ask, but I am worried about getting dirt on our new furniture." You would be respectful.

There are three parts to an effective "I" statement: the annoying behavior, how you feel, and why you feel that way. Dr. Gordon says the "why" part is the most important and the one parents leave out the most. An example from my family was when my son was riding his tricycle in the house. It's not enough to say, "I don't like when you ride the tricycle in the house." It needs to be "I don't like when you ride the tricycle in the house, because you might run into the walls or run over your sister's foot." Phrasing it like this also turns the problem over to the child to solve. A negotiation might be workable such that the child figures out a way to ride the tricycle without bumping into walls or his sister.

Dr. Gordon warns against "sending a solution" to children when you state your problem. He writes, "All the following types of messages 'send a solution': 1. ORDERING, DIRECTING, COMMANDING 'You go find something to play with'" (ch. 6).

This helped me as an adult even, especially in my marriage. How many times did I do the cliché thing of telling my husband "Well, go do whatever you want!" or something like it. Now I don't. This is commanding a solution. Instead, I feel the urge to lash out, blame him, or "send a solution" rise in me, but I don't do these things. I sit through the pain I am feeling. I trust that stating my true feelings will air them and, in time, a solution will be found through mutual problem-solving.

I found that a very effective way to model "I" statements with toddlers is in how you thank them. Instead of just saying "Thank you," be very specific about what you are thanking them for. I found my children picked up on this easily and started doing it. They did it with everyone, including strangers, and it was adorable when they would very specifically thank strangers, e.g., "Thank you very much for holding the door open for me."

Dr. Gordon's *Parent Effectiveness Training* discusses resolving conflict in a house through brainstorming and negotiation. Brainstorming and negotiation are what you do if the needs of the parent and the needs of the child conflict. It's what you do when a mere "I" statement doesn't work to resolve the conflict. Brainstorming isn't possible with a toddler. I found they are capable of this at the milestone that starts at the age of five years and that I named "Negotiation and Reasonableness." When needs conflict with a toddler, different approaches are needed. At each milestone in Section Two, I give further ideas of how to gain a child's cooperation. And, thus, the only point I want to make in this chapter is that "I" statements are not always going to achieve a workable outcome. A child might hear what you are saying and understand it, but there are 820 reasons why they might not want to comply. I only point this out so you don't get discouraged if an "I" statement doesn't work for you at a moment when you are hoping it will.

It is one of my deepest wishes that more people would get good at conflict resolution. I structured this book to have a "Conflict Resolution" section instead of "Discipline" in part to highlight how important this skill set is. I wish people would realize what is their problem and what is not. I once was trying to get my family ready to leave the house for an outing. A visitor started in on high-pressure tactics to get my son ready, which didn't work. I was busy and after I came in, I easily got him ready. After this, the *visitor* wasn't ready to depart. We had to wait another 15 minutes for this person to get ready. Our trip would have gone so much more smoothly if they had just worried about their own problems. I wish people would realize that if they insert themselves into another's problem, they can only be effective after they've extended ample empathy to the other person and gotten to know that person's situation, much like a doctor evaluating a patient.

If you were to take an inventory of behaviors you find unacceptable and ask any other caregiver of your child to do the same, you are certain to find that the lists are very different. I once saw a child climb a tree. I was admiring his athletic talent. Another adult chased the child away from the tree, yelling at him for being "disrespectful" to the tree. It doesn't mean that either adult is "wrong" because they have different values and different permissible actions. (This is why I am opposed to putting up a "united front." It is ok to have different tolerances and different solutions under each caregiver.) You have a right not to be Ok with certain behaviors, but you then also have the responsibility to address them. I encourage others to confront my children if there is a conflict, but to do it *respectfully*. Before inserting yourself to confront the child, please answer this question: How does the situation and its outcome affect you? Why is it a bother to you? And communicate that exact thing to the child.

Give Information

I learned about the approach of "give information" from Dr. Ginott, who says, "The easiest way to make children feel that there is something wrong with them is to criticize. It diminishes their image of themselves. Instead of criticism, children need information without derogation" (ch. 4).

Informative statements are used to bring the child's awareness to the function of an object when they are using an object improperly, say standing on the backrest of the couch. You might tell them, "The couch is for sitting." At the very last milestone in the toddler years, Toddler Milestone 12, this becomes effective. The toddler becomes very interested in how to use things and picking what tool works for what job. I would tell my daughter at this age "Blankets belong inside," and she would usually comply.

My husband once told my son, then about three years old, why pulling on the miniblinds in the way my son was doing it could harm them. I didn't even know what he had taught. I had pulled on the miniblinds in an incorrect way. I benefited from this approach!

In the late twos, children follow instructions much better. I was able to tell my daughter, "The safe spot is the sidewalk," meaning that after she was out of her car seat that she should stand on the sidewalk to wait while I got her infant brother out of the van. This is a clear expectation. When children are running off, ask: Have you stated to them your expectation? Do they know how to behave or what is expected of them? They need clear information to know what you expect.

Give a Lesson

I found that from the late twos, all throughout the threes and fours, children become very interested in right versus wrong. Dr. Gordon writes to not "send a solution" to children. He also writes against family meetings which can feel like a "sermon." I wasn't sure where this tactic of giving children a lesson might play a role, given the good doctor's warnings about not "sending a solution." However, I think giving a *lesson* and giving a *lecture* are fundamentally different. It's the difference between sitting down and giving a lesson that simply illuminates ideal/less-than-ideal behavior versus yelling at a kid "Just go outside and play!" when an adult is annoyed with them. It's the difference between an approach which feels like, "Here is a lesson about right versus wrong behavior that will likely help you have better knowledge, make better decisions, and also may help our family" versus "You're irritating and need to change." Dr. Gordon says he supports "brainstorming sessions" where family members are encouraged to put issues on a white board and discuss and negotiate them at regular intervals. This can be considered a "family meeting," but it doesn't have the "You kids sit down and hear what your mother and I have to say" vibe to it that he warns about it. There are ways to give healthy lessons and have healthy meetings.

I often gave lessons to my kids especially at these ages. Conflicts arose often enough that I started to get good at doing a lesson on the spot. My favorite type of lesson at the toddler age is to retell the events of what happened. Then after this, I show a better way to get what they were trying to get. I find children love to be the star of such a "play."

I strongly favored lessons like this until shortly after age 5. At age 5, children are much more capable of negotiation and don't need quite as many lessons like this, as simple explanations work well. However, such formal lessons may help, even into the teenage years or adult years. For instance, if your teenager is driving your car, do you maybe want them to know how to handle a flat tire? You'll need to give a lesson. And giving this lesson can reduce the likelihood of a volatile situation later when they are out and get a flat tire (and may cause the parents to explode with anger). The more technical information children have, the better decisions they can make, and the less likely volatile situations will erupt. I see clearly how having both technical skills and having emotional intelligence/negotiation skills strengthen and improve each other. Let's put to rest this idea that parents should not teach their children things, as if all of it is bound to be just lecturing sermons that don't go anywhere. Let's instead get good at teaching.

I won't specifically tell you to "lower your expectations" as a parent. If you want to have fine china out on display and teach your kids to not break it, that's up to you. But, one should expect that enforcing any of what is required to accomplish that goal will require effort. My approach is to have low expectations but to handle those conflicts wisely and well.

Teaching: A Gift, Not a Gauntlet

In many parenting books, there is a usual emotion/teaching dichotomy. Those on the "emotion" side tend to think that "tools" to use with children are not authentic, that lessons are futile, and the best thing one can do is set an example. On the "teaching" side of the dichotomy are thinkers who are often dismissive of emotions, perhaps telling adults or children to get a grip and stop whining. The underlying belief of both sides is that receiving a lesson is bound to be an awful, grating experience. Thus, don't do it (the progressive side) or lean in harder with little care for the proper care of the child for the sake of performance (the traditional side). This can be rectified if people learn how to be better teachers.

I would like to make a case that *parents* should become good at teaching, a case that I'll start with a story. Once, my son, who was four, wanted to put garland on the rail of our staircase. Instead of outright telling him "No," I told him, "I am worried the garland will scratch the wood," which happened the last time he had done that. To my astonishment, he weaved the garland through the metal (not the wood) part of the rails on the staircase! I had previously given him lessons on the difference between wood, metal, plastic, glass, and rubber—and here he was using the information to resolve a conflict! Actively teaching my children as much as I can has helped our household much. If, when your child is 16, and you may want to teach him or her a few things as you hand the keys to your car over, you may wish to have invested in knowing how to teach.

The problem with teaching today is that it is overbearing, demanding, critical, and lecturing. My experience is that adults ask too many questions of children, are too quick to interfere and correct a child, and they try to force children into activities they clearly are not interested in. Children become defiant, impatient, and angry. Perhaps not knowing any better method, some caregivers say, "Aww, to hell with any of it!"

If I had to describe the problem simply, it is that too many, including those in formal education positions themselves, go straight to testing without much teaching. Quality teaching is seen as "cheating" or "spoon feeding" children. Adults ask too many questions of the children right away, expecting them to know the answer after receiving only a brief explanation—or in some cases, no explanation at all. Looking up answers is considered cheating, collaborating with others is considered cheating, any type of struggle is seen as laziness. Tell me: Are these the way that a typical profession operates, where you cannot look up answers or collaborate with others?

On the other side of this, but less frequent, are adults who actively let their children struggle through problems, without correcting the child, but to the point of letting the child flounder. I am opposed to this too. With the understanding of the regressive/progressive nature of cognitive growth spurts, I expect this will start to resolve as well. For instance, the *Wall Street Journal* had an article, "What Teens Need Most from Their Parents." This article outlined typical development of teenagers, and, in their research, it is clear they found cognitive growth spurts. Consider this about 11-year-olds:

> As puberty takes center stage, tweens can actually slip backward in some basic skills. Spatial learning and certain kinds of reasoning may decline at this stage, studies show. Parts of the brain responsible for prospective memory, or remembering what you are supposed to do in the future, are still maturing. This may be why a teen may seem clueless if asked to give the teacher a note before school. (Shellenbarger)

This is a cognitive growth spurt. (It is likely a cluster of them in succession.) If you know this is happening, it becomes futile and almost cruel to punish the child for it. It becomes futile also to let the children "experience the natural consequences" of their actions when they forget the note to school and miss a field trip. This is what I mean by letting a child flounder.

I am opposed to using "natural consequences" as a teaching tool. I have no problem with letting children feel the consequences of their actions, but it is not a *teaching* tool. If, for instance, you want your child to understand that not studying leads to a bad grade, you cannot think, "Well I won't intervene. They will fail, and they will learn a lesson." This may or may not be the lesson learned. One lesson may be that the child instead learns to cheat in order to pass the test. Natural consequences are healthy and necessary but accept that the lessons that your child learns via their own personal experience every single minute of every single day as they navigate the world are highly personal, private,—and completely awesome. It is a process that you have no control over.

I see too much faith in the power of natural consequences sometimes in parents of toddlers also. As parents potty train, they might let children go without a diaper in hopes that they won't like soiling themselves and will use the potty. My experience is that children often don't care if they are soiled. They get messy and they just live with it. If you want to actively teach something, it needs to be *taught*. As the subtitle of the *Wall Street Journal* article concludes about teenagers, "They need coaching, support, good examples and most of all understanding." Children need guidance and support from young ages all the way through the teenage years. In fact, adults need it as well, all the way through the rest of life. People need mentors.

The point I want to hammer on is that teaching should be clear and simple. It should not be the confusing gauntlet that it is now, where children are expected to jump through hoops to get information, as if it is a test of them. Teachers should take pride in what they awaken in their students, not in how difficult their class is. From Dr. Sheldon Margulies at FascinatingEducation.com, who teaches advanced science concepts using crystal clear visuals, "If a student doesn't understand, it's on me, because I'm not explaining it properly."

Giving a proper lesson to a child should not be a sermon either. Nothing about how you approach it should be "You are wrong, I am right, and sit down while I explain that to you." If this sting is removed from teaching, I think more and more people would be on board that teaching is not necessarily an awful, emotionally invalidating, sermonizing experience.

Because of the lecturing awfulness of some teaching, I think many are opposed to early academics. I am, however, a fan of early academics; yes, even with a 1½ year old. The benefits of early education are many. For one, a bigger vocabulary helps with communication. And it's not just math or reading you can teach them, but social skills and etiquette as well. Most importantly, the children are flexing their brain "muscle."

Sure, most of the day for a toddler can be spent doing free play. I strive for one lesson a day with a child so young, which takes maybe 5 minutes, depending on the lesson. I use methods that are the very first stages of Montessori with toddlers—a lot of matching games and a lot of pointing to things—which proved powerful, especially for vocabulary building. I taught both of my older children to count to 100 by the time they were 3, my daughter to read, and many other skills. My primary goal when I teach is clarity—all fun and playful ways to approach it are a delight but secondary.

Three Stages of Learning

I rely heavily on the three stages of learning in my teaching, which I learned from Dr. Maria Montessori. For example, to teach basic words using a picture book, I would first point to a picture and say what it is (stage one). I linger here for a while. When I am ready to move on, I repeat stage one, and then I immediately ask if they can point to that object (stage two). Then, after much practice, I may ask them "What is this?" where they tell me what it is (stage three). The stages progress in difficulty from simple demonstration (stage one) to a "multiple choice" question (stage two) to an open-ended question (stage three). It is a very simple and straightforward way with no tricks or needless complexity. The first stage is a demonstration and the last two are an assessment. The last two stages also serve as practice. Stage two is a little easier to give an assist. It is necessary for the learning process as it asks the child to recall the information, which is necessary for the information to stick. When you first meet someone and they tell you their name, it is best to repeat it back to yourself to remember it. Similarly, the child learns by being asked a very simple question of him or her about the material.

The last two stages of learning are necessary for the actual learning process, but children should not be pushed if they struggle when they get to them. I often jumped around in the stages as I taught, based on how well my child was responding. If at any time a child doesn't respond as expected, the lesson ends. In The Montessori Method, the "directress," in your case, parent, is discouraged from repeating the lesson, as it was already given. Doing the same thing twice in a row will not likely get a different result. Simply try it at a different time.

In approaching the learning of vocabulary this way, my children learned new words easily. It also set the stage for what I call stage four, where children notice objects in the world around them. One of the greatest aspects of the Montessori system is how children develop skills spontaneously. I was thrilled when, after reading many picture books with a moon in it, my son, as a toddler, would, on his own initiative, point to the real one in the sky and say, "Moon!" In fact, he seemed to catch it right when the sun set and was first visible. Using these stages of learning caused my children to be very astute observers of daily life.

For many concepts, particularly attributes of objects, e.g., color and shape, the approach is a little different. Before telling the child the name of the attribute, it is best to have the child work with the attribute. For instance, with colors, it is best to have the child play matching games with colors, developing awareness and interest in colors. Simply have objects that are identical except color and have the child sort them by color. Do this by showing children what to do with few words. Then after they can do this, showing they are capable of understanding color, take them through the three stages of learning. I found it best to do three colors at a time and to do strongly contrasting ones first. After they sort the colors, point to the color and say what it is. Then ask, "Which one is red?" Then "What color is this?" When I used this approach to teach colors, my children at those ages again would see colors, spontaneously point to them, and say, "This is green!" How wonderful it is to see your child voluntarily challenging themselves to name the color of objects all around them!

Teaching width and length is similar. After a child works with the knobbed cylinders, you can teach for instance "short" and "tall." Take the shortest cylinder and say, "This is short." Take the tallest cylinder and say, "This is tall."

This approach, using the three stages of learning, dominates much of my teaching. I always present opposites and a continuum if possible. In the same way that I always teach short as compared to tall, I teach "insulates" and "conducts" when I do science experiments with my children. I teach "discourage" along with "courage" when I teach these traits. If possible, I teach a continuum. For instance, when teaching emotions, to teach "angry," I present several words: annoyed, irritated, angry, and infuriated. I loosely think of this as the "Three Little Bears" principle. Something about teaching "cold, warm, hot" appeals to children greatly. Any lesson presented to the child should be conceptually clear.

I also found it was often best to wait one night after a demonstration before asking any questions of the child. Depending on the complexity of the lesson, I would give the lesson, and wait until the next day to ask any questions. Something about the overnight sleep helped the child's understanding. I write, "DO NOT ASK QUESTIONS" right on the document where I plan lessons as a reminder to myself, as it is always tempting to ask the child questions. I always wanted to know if what I said "stuck" or not. It's so disappointing not to know if your lesson resonated with your child. I found it almost always did, and I just had to give it time for my child to reveal they understood.

Encouraging Observation (Achieving Sensory Education)

To promote spontaneous observation of daily life, Montessori also has the children do memory games. For instance, with the color tablets, the "directress" may show the child a particular color tablet and ask the child to retrieve its match in the next room. The child must remember the task at hand while going to the next room and retain an image in mind of what the color looks like. This helps to extend the children's memory of colors such that, after their lessons, as they go about daily life, they can remember which color is which, even the most nuanced shades of color.

Asking the child to color something also serves as an activity to notice more about reality. Try it yourself. Pick a coloring book of real things and try to color it in. You may find you notice a lot more detail about that object.

Montessori writes that many people graduate college and enter a profession, but require years if not decades before finally becoming good at what they do. Most people think that a person needs experience until they are good at a job. Montessori puts forth the idea that if the person had a quality sensory education, they would not need these years of experience to become competent at a job. Experience is important, of course, and people who are truly good at something always have ample experience with it—it's the years of being unproductive as one learns the basics that are being addressed. If a person did not have a sensory education, they must spend years until they become accustomed to the observations required in their profession. A chef must learn what meat looks like when it is cooked properly just as a physician must learn what an illness looks like. A sensory education encourages a child to become sensitive to the meta-properties that make up all objects, thus giving the child the sharpest pair of epistemological glasses possible. (Epistemology is the study of the acquiring of knowledge.) They do not become astute observers of only those things in a particular field, but of all things everywhere. This is why I've come to see a sensory education as the ultimate preparatory work.

Control of Error

The other genius of the Montessori system is that the materials have a built-in control to them such that children can see for themselves if they made an error. When doing the knobbed cylinders, for instance, the cylinders can only be inserted correctly in one way. If the child gets it wrong, the child can see very clearly that a thick cylinder does not fit in a thin hole. The child is thus inspired to keep going until it is right. An adult does not have to make corrections, because the material does.

I use this notion of error control in all my teaching. I give children the answer right away. For instance, when my son was 5, I gave him a 10X10 grid on which to write the numbers 1 – 100. I sat down to do it with him. When I filled in mine, he said, "Oh! Thank you! This shows me how to do it!" He was grateful, and it did not cause him to give up because he knew the answer. Even having the answers, he still struggled. He once skipped a number, noticed it, and crumpled up his paper. My inclination was to assure him it was ok, but I stopped myself. He simply got another grid paper and started over. After this lesson, he became fascinated with numbers bigger than 100. He read them everywhere, such as the year on calendars or addresses. Had I made him complete the 10X10 grid without the assist, how much time would be wasted being confused about numbers, when his mind could have otherwise been occupied, such as it was, for example, with how long ago Julius Caesar lived or how big numbers could go?

After I give lessons, I let my children spontaneously do what they want with the information. In fact, many of my lesson ideas spring forth from simply watching what my children were naturally interested in. I let them repeat what they want over and over. I loosely consider the Montessori approach as "intellectual gymnastics." In the same way that a sports coach gives a demonstration and then let players practice until they develop mastery, in the Montessori system, children are given lessons and repeat them to gain intellectual mastery. I used to be confused on when to help children or not, but the answer is simple: If they ask for help, give it in a straightforward manner. If they don't ask, let them persist in their work.

Learning by Doing

To teach discipline, true to the idea that people learn best by doing, Montessori advocates discipline through doing. It is not enough, she writes, simply to ask children not to touch the flowers. Instead, she gets them involved in the care and maintenance of flowers. In this way, they learn to treat this very interesting object in the correct way. As they watch the miracle of life grow before their eyes, they take pride in what they have helped grow and would not harm it. To learn how to be quiet, the children are not just told to sit still. Instead, they do exercises where they move quietly, such as moving silently to the back of a room after their name is called. It is a game to the children and they take great enjoyment and pride in accomplishing it. I extend this at home. To encourage ideal behavior, we practice the ideal behavior. For instance, if I want my toddler to walk on the sidewalk and not run on to the road, we walk on the sidewalk, and I gently move them to the sidewalk every time they stray. This is true to the "gymnastics" approach in that it is learning through repetitive action. I also let my children use the garbage can as a garbage can, letting them throw away actual garbage.

In reading about Montessori, I have also adopted these principles into my life. If I am about to do an activity where I need to think on the spot, I will practice what I am about to do several times before doing it. This increases my ability to observe what is critical quickly. Seems like such a simple idea, right? Most good ideas are. Isolating out this best practice as a concept allows me to think of it in every situation where it may be useful.

In fact, the very act of writing this chapter is a form of practice. By writing about her ideas, I can contemplate further the thoughts presented by Montessori. This activity caused me to have many more insights about it than had I simply read her work.

Lessons as an Act of Focused Love

I strive to do one lesson per day for each of my children. On a weekly basis, I sit down and think of lessons for each of my children. I have found this acted as a form of meditation. In doing this, it focused me on each of them, their unique talents, and where they were at in their development. As I approached them the next day, I was a more astute observer of them. I found that if I wasn't planning lessons like this, I was more likely to get irritated with my children. But if I was planning lessons, I noticed more, and I felt more in love with them. If I was involved like this, I would go to sleep more often thinking of their latest development and with a big happy smile. This is in alignment with the Montessori idea of preparing a person to be an observer of life. It requires preparatory work. Making lessons and documenting my children acted as this preparatory work.

I also found I never really felt like my children's childhood was passing me by too quickly. Certainly, I get nostalgic every now and then. Once, when my children were away, I saw toys on the floor and the emotion overwhelmed me that the toys had no real meaning unless my children were playing with them—and this would be the eventual fate of the toys. However, this feeling was a mixture of sad and happy. I do not feel like I am missing any stage or like my children will be "gone" someday. I recognize that they will become adults, but they are still my children. I see it simply as a different stage, and we'll have a different relationship. I know what each of the milestones is, and I can tell you the activities my children loved best at those milestones.

I thus encourage you to journal your children and plan lessons. Perhaps for each milestone—markers on a great journey—take note of their favorite activity and/or take a picture as you engage them. I know many of my readers are very crafty and could take this idea far further! The benefits of this, while they go towards the valuable end of teaching your child, extend far greater.

A Child's Fear of Abandonment

I was once struck upon reading that, universally, children have a fear of abandonment. I have dealt with this issue with my toddlers and preschoolers so many times. I was very comforted to learn that this is something that just seems to be "in" children. I collected the unexpected ways that this shows up when you parent, and how you sometimes must tread carefully to avoid flare-ups.

Garbage Cans, Drains, Give Away Piles

One of my most heartbreaking moments as a parent is when my son noticed the water draining in the bathtub. I was excited to teach him the idea of "draining," and how the water was going away, down a pipe. As the water went down, he said, "And now John will go away." Oh my!!! Tears! Sad tears!

We went through and Konmari'd our house once. The Konmari system of organization is outlined by Marie Kondo in her book *The Life-Changing Magic of Tidying Up: The Japanese Art of Decluttering and Organizing*. Her approach focuses on getting rid of anything that does not "spark joy" for a person. We went to Goodwill about 15 times, taking 30-45 bins worth of stuff. My son, who was 3, told us once, "I had a nightmare that you dropped me off at Goodwill." These moments kill me.

It is so important to deal with things that "go away" from your house. This issue of abandonment is so big, it is worth it to preface to children that they will not be given away whenever explaining drains, garbage cans, and the like.

Minor Separations

I was with my 4-year-old and two other family members at a bookstore once. I took my 4-year-old to the bathroom. The two other family members left towards the front entrance. When my son got out of the bathroom, he bolted to find them. This left us in a panic as he ran through the store. Several weeks later, he broke out into tears. He said, "Do you remember when [the two other family members] left me behind?" He had been full of fear of abandonment when he didn't see them upon returning from the bathroom.

Now if we have a brief separation, we agree on a place to meet up. The fear of abandonment is that deep.

Bedtime

I have read before that the most traumatic part of the day for a child is when you leave their side at bedtime. Certainly, parents have had bedtime struggles where a child keeps getting out of bed. If this happens, I would encourage any parent to first see if there is an unmet need of the child. The very first place I would look is to food and mealtimes. When we switched over to routine meal times, where food is served family style at regular, predictable times, our bedtime struggles were greatly relieved. But another potential unmet need may be that the child needs connection.

Bedtimes can be a struggle and in getting the child to do as asked, a parent may fall into a trap of, "If you don't [brush your teeth, go to the potty, etc.], I am going to leave." It can be super rough to tough it out with a child who is being uncooperative, but what should never, ever be compromised is connection right before they go to bed. Dr. Ginott describes how parents need to be there to talk through any anxiety or fears a child has, so they can lull the child to sleep. We do a happy/sad part of the day every single night. I will never not do this. No lectures allowed at this time, just a genuine discussion of emotion. It is OK to leave the child at bedtime during particularly rough nights, but avoid saying it such as "Fine! I'm leaving!" Instead it needs to be a kind but firm departure. When my daughter was almost three years old, I found that when I would let her snuggle with me for a few minutes before bed, she willingly got into her bed. I wish sometimes that we had bigger beds such that I could simply cuddle with my toddler children as they went to sleep, something which I know many parents do. Singing to them before you leave is a nice connection that may lull them to sleep.

Hellos and Goodbyes

It is of no surprise to any parent that hellos and especially goodbyes can trigger fear in children. Parents' first drop off at school can be filled with anxiety. Children panic when their mom tries to slip away for an appointment or a much-needed date night.

I make it a point when saying hello or goodbye to my children, that we always connect. It's, "Hello! It's nice to see you!" It's never, "Hello. Did you dress properly today? Did you behave at school?" Or when we say goodbye, it's, "I hope you have a fun time!" It's never, "Be sure to behave!" All the coaching and guidance stuff can come at other times. At these critical hi/bye times, it is important to connect.

Who Helps Them

I've yet to figure this one out. My children, during the toddler and preschool years, would often demand that I, and only I, help them at certain times. One time, my son, who was four at the time, was crying for me to help him out of his car seat. I decided to leave him in the van, as his dad would help him, and I left with his sister. Partially, I was tired of this happening and partially I wanted to see what happened. My son, in hysterics, said, "Mommy is leaving me!" There is clearly some kind of fear of abandonment at play.

There are many other situations to be mindful of in which this fear of abandonment may apply. One major one is moving to a new house. I am also very careful in how I speak. I never will say something like, "I'm leaving now! I'll leave without you if you don't hurry up!" Never. Ever. The fear of abandonment is so big, this is never something to say. I am completely aghast when I hear stories of parents dropping their kids off at the side of the street as a form of punishment.

Parenting is through thick and thin. You must be there for your kid, not abandoning them, even when they are annoying, crying, grumpy, uncooperative, doing bad at school, going through puberty, and so on. This issue has been a mystery to me for some time: Why would nature make children so frustrating at times, making parents want to turn away, when the children's real need is for parents to come closer? It truly highlights the reality that parents must have a principled, values-based approach to what they do.

.

A Child's Need for Connection

From my reading and research, it is clear to me that children need lots of connection from other humans in the way of emotional presence, stimulating activities, friendship, and physical contact. I often wonder how this developed and how humans of the past handled this, as it is apparent that modern humans suffer from lack of connection (more so or less depending on the culture). Trying to understand this, I have noticed two things: (1) Other children are remarkably good at providing connection to other children and (2) adults often stop it. This second observation is a result of living and being in various places across the United States.

I realized this when my infant son was going through an infant "leap." My infant was up late, screaming. I was with him, trying to calm him down. My 5-year-old had been put to bed already, but he got up to be in the room where I was with his younger brother. At first, I was annoyed by this. I had already put him to bed and I didn't want to do it again. Further, he was all over his infant brother somewhat like he was trying to poke him. I realized, however, that my 5-year-old was doing exactly what I propose people do with a child at these times—connect with them. I thought to myself, "Why am I fighting this? Why don't I let my five-year-old deal with my infant while I go get a late-night cup of coffee?" Ok, the late-night coffee never happened.

My 5-year-old had a remarkable ability to provide support to his infant brother at many stages of development. Once, he saw my infant trying to stand up, and he came over and simply picked him up. As my 5-year-old did this, I knew that if certain adults had seen it, they would have ordered him to stop. It would have been seen as careless or that he would hurt my infant. And, yet, my infant did not get hurt and was greatly benefited by his supportive big brother there to help him stand up.

I have been in so many situations where children go to connect with each other and adults stop it. Once, my daughter, age 2 at the time, sat on the top of a slide. Another girl of a similar age came to sit next to her. What I saw, as I looked at the two girls, were two children in the sun, simply enjoying each other's presence. There were few other people at the playground, and the children were not stopping anyone from using the slide. The other girl's caregiver came over to say, "Come on, you go down the slide," and effectively pushed her to go down.

Another time, I was at the playground again and my daughter, still age 2, was on top of some of the equipment. A boy, about six-years old, was interested in her. He was near her, simply playing with mulch as he looked at her. An adult, I am assuming his mother, said, "He is being a creepers!" and moved him away from my daughter, despite my protests that he was fine. In the moment, I was livid that this boy, who was such a young boy, had been called a "creepers," as if a young boy simply wanting to play with a young girl made him sexually exploitive or weird.

This is a story from my personal notes of some scowling adults and the good that they could have stopped had the children not been allowed to connect, in the messy way that children tend to connect:

At baseball tonight, Emily started interacting with some other children. I wish you could have seen the scowls on some of the adults' faces as the children interacted. By nature, children are just a little unrefined in how they do things, and they get sneers from adults. Really. It happens.

At one point, Emily started to put what she was eating to one of the boy's lips. I did not intervene. I was with my infant, thus mostly distracted, but I usually don't intervene unless a child is upset. My husband went over to ask her to not put the food to the boy's lips.

To my mind, I would think that this pro-active move on my husband's part would relieve the scowls. They instead got worse. He came back over to me. Really, the judgment from other adults was palpable. He said to me, I think sensing how the adults were reacting, "I feel bad that she is taunting that boy."

I said, "She is taunting that boy? *That* boy? That boy followed me around at the playground during the last game to tell me about how he lost a tooth that day and his mom calls him a Master Builder at LEGO's. That boy is not feeling taunted right now. I don't see children taunting each other. I see children connecting."

A few minutes later, one of the older girls approached Emily. I thought to myself, "Oh boy. Something happened. Emily is being confronted. Well whatever it is, I'll deal with it."

The girl said, "Emily, could you ask your mom if you can come to the playground with us?"

I looked at my husband, gave a quick raised eyebrow and smile and said, "Emily just got invited to play with them."

They went to a nearby field. All the other children were probably eight years old or over. The children organized a game and Emily took directions from them. They rounded her up when she went astray. They comforted her when she seemed confused. It was beautiful. We watched, somewhat far away, as our daughter made friends and played, in the middle of a field, on a beautiful night. This is the *stuff childhood is made of.* My husband teared up as he watched it.

Note: My husband tells me he felt bad for the boy, because he wasn't allowed to have food and my daughter was eating some in front of him and trying to give him some. Nonetheless, it was the pressure from other adults that made him feel bad.

I give my children an enormous amount of freedom to connect with each other. There are times that extending this freedom to my children makes my heart skip a beat and not in a good way. My 5-year-old would come up to my infant sometimes and shake his arms back and forth, such that my overly sensitive thought was that my infant's arms might break. And yet, my infant would laugh uproariously over it. I can't argue with giggles. When my children (at young ages) get into conflict, I have a 30-second rule. Unless one of them is in obvious pain, I let them try to resolve the conflict before I step in. I do keep tabs on them. I ask, "Is this fun or not fun?" Or I sometimes ask, "Did you do that in anger or for fun?" If it's for fun, I let it continue. If it's out of anger, we talk about it.

Recent studies have found that the best predictor for good sibling relationships later in life is how much fun the kids have together when they're young. The rate of conflict can even be high, as long as there's plenty of fun to balance it out. The real danger comes when the siblings just ignore each other. (Siegel and Bryson, ch. 6)

I get in the way sometimes. One time, my toddler daughter was sandwiching my 5-year-old son in a beach chair that folds. I told her to stop. My son said, "Mommy, I like when she smooshes me." My bad. I thanked him for telling me what his boundary was. On with the smooshing.

Here is another story from my personal notes of a time that not intervening worked well:

We went to a botanical garden yesterday. They have a children's area. I was with Emily (2, almost three years old). The parents there had a pretty bad case of yelling. There were older kids there, all soaking wet, and it was a lot of, "Did you just put that in your mouth!? What's wrong with you!?" "Why? WHY? Why are you doing that?" "GET. OFF. I SAID. GET. OFF." "Don't sit on the rocks!" (to a girl already soaked and dirty). Oh, of course, "You're walking home!" It's cool. I should have empathy that they lack the skill set to deal effectively with their children, and I should not be judgmental.

Anyway, Emily was playing on this rock that had water bubbling out of it. Another girl, about 9 or 10, was there. Emily had pushed the girl away. The other girl said, "No pushing." I did not intervene. And as the parents sat, hovering, wanting to yell, but didn't, because it was not their child, I was prepared to say the following:

"I see a girl who was asked not to push and complied."

I didn't have to say that, as no one confronted me. And immediately after watching me have a watchful eye on my daughter but not intervening, resulting in the children playing cooperatively, all their attitudes changed. It was a lot of, "Oh, they are so cute."

I flatter myself that my presence and attitude changed the yelling, a negative, into noticing and celebrating children, a positive.

I'm not denying that adults need to have an active presence and influence in children's lives. When conflict breaks out, adults need to be there to help sort through the issue, including the emotions of the children, what it is they are fighting over, and give them better ways to deal with it. But adults get in the way big time. It's the sneering, the insults, the yelling, the sermonizing that I have a problem with. My biggest challenge as a parent is not how to handle my children. It is how to handle adults who are like this. I find when adults are like this, their rage sometimes transfers to me, and I can feel the rage inside of me: emotions are contagious! It can be very hard at times to manage my own emotions and the deal with my children—work which seems to appear all but invisible to others—and when I am exposed to a bunch of toxic judgments from someone else, ordering me to "get my children in line," after an unexpected flare up, it is often more than I can bear. I need the grace of at least a few minutes to deal with it, and I often don't get this simple courtesy. Kids are messy. They make mistakes. I'd like to see more people understand that and deal with it in understanding, supportive, and even playful ways. Misbehavior is growth!

I think deep down many parents want to connect with their children and give them room to make mistakes and handle conflict, but the pressure from others to conform immediately causes parents to act in ways they don't want to. I think many times that adults lash out at children, it is not because of the child, but is due to pressure on parents from other adults.

I do not believe this is how humans thrive best or even what was the natural development over the course of human history. An active effort disrupted it. Dr. Ashley Montagu writes in *Touching: The Human Significance of the Skin* that a movement to limit physical contact—that such contact "spoils" a child—began in the late 1800s and has had negative effects since its inception. It is why some people throughout the twentieth century thought breastfeeding was gross or likely cannot tolerate whatsoever the sight of a breastfeeding mother. This greatly affects the type of people that children grow up to be and not for the better. Consider his profound insight into how it affected music as the effects spread:

> It has been said that music utters the things that cannot be spoken. In much music there is a very pervasive tactile quality. Wagner's "Liebestod" is said to represent a musical version of coitus leading to orgasm and postcoital subsidence. Debussy's "L'Apres-Midi d'un Faune" conveys the most tactile of sexual nuances. In the "rock" music of our day, so aptly named, for the first time in the history of the dance in the Western world the participating couples no longer touch each other at any time but remain separated throughout the dance, dancing most of the time to deafeningly loud music of which the lyrics, usually addressed to one's parents, or generally to the older generation, only too often say, "You do not understand," "Where were you when I needed you?" or words to that effect.

> [C]an it be that dances like the Twist and later ones of the same rock variety, together with rock music, represent, at least in part, reactions to a lack of early tactile stimulation, to a deprivation suffered in the antiseptic, dehumanized environments created by obstetricians and hospitals? Where but in such a setting should we enact this most important of all dramatic events: the birth and welcoming of a new member into "the bosom of the family?" (172-173)

I do what is in my power to counter the lack of connection and to attempt to connect authentically with people I meet outside of my family. When out, I actively smile at people. It greatly reduces potential tension. I hate being an anonymous face anywhere. It is so much more likely that toxic blame gets laid at my feet if I am an anonymous face. I won't go to crowded places where children are allowed to play because of it, such as an indoor playground. I actively build relationships, and I strongly prefer to be in places where people know us.

I would love to see a book about how to have positive, healthy touch with children, for instance how to make bath time go well or how to brush a child's hair in a soothing manner. I can see how something as simple as how you brush a child's hair can affect the kind of touch they will come to expect.

To encourage more connection during everyday events, I put together this short list of ways that everyday interactions with your child can be turned into a more positive interaction. These are things I learned the hard way. This is the level of detail I personally needed to make these normal things, such as giving a child a bath, go well. I don't doubt another person can come up with a much better list and expand on this greatly, perhaps into its own book. I would gladly read it!

Ways to Make Everyday Events More Pleasant

Before putting lotion on a child, warm it up in your hand so it is not cold. Do the same with soap.

A good shampoo makes a big difference to get tangles out before you go to brush a child's hair.

The most tear-free way to brush hair is to start at the bottom and work your way up. A pick or comb is best on wet hair and a brush on dry hair.

Products such as a "Tear Free Rinser" can be used to help wash soap or shampoo out of a child's hair. It fits around the child's forehead so water falls away from the eyes.

Use proper tools helps with grooming chores, such as using fingernail clippers designed for children.

Eating Together as an Act of Presence and Love

I'll be the first to tell you that I am not a food expert, or a cooking expert, or a getting kids to eat expert. After reading several books on nutrition, digestive health problems, and approaches to serving food to children, I thought that providing parents with an overview of the different thoughts and approaches may be helpful.

The three approaches I am going to review are:
1) The "French" way
2) The Division of Responsibility
3) Let them do it themselves

The French Way

The "French" way was made popular by the book *French Kids Eat Everything*. I use the word "French" loosely. I can appreciate that it is unlikely that every person in France follows the approach put forward, but, loosely, I call it "the French way." The author, Karen Le Billon, articulates her experiences of living in France for a year. The approach described is one of "gentle authoritarianism." Children come to the table at prescribed times; they do not eat in between; the children are made to eat what is on the menu; they are fed by an adult; they sometimes are screaming for food; and a chef is provided at every school to cook meals.

Division of Responsibility

The "Division of Responsibility" was developed by Ellen Satyr. I learned it from the book *Help Your Child with Extreme Picky Eating* (Rowell, McGlothlin and Evans Morris). Food is served family style at the table. Dishes with food are set out at the table for everyone to help themselves. Children are discouraged from eating in between meal times. At least one "safe" food should be served: something you know the child will like. Ellen Satyr's website describes this approach where the "parent is responsible for what, when, where" and "the child is responsible for how much and whether."

Let Them Do It Themselves

In *Positive Discipline A-Z*, the authors recommend as one suggestion, "Some families allow children to make themselves a sandwich or tortilla with cheese if they don't like the meal. This is better than cooking special dishes for each child" (Nelsen, Lott and Glenn, "Eating and Mealtime Hassles").

These are the three methods with which I am familiar. When I look at them, one thing I notice is the theme of presence. I think of the theme I gave to this book, which is presence, and its importance. In the first two methods, presence of food is abundant, whether children are having it jammed down their throat or picking it out themselves. A seasoned mother once said to me that she thought the best thing you could do to promote healthy eating is to simply "place food in front of children." She described how this was the way her upbringing was and that she remembers thinking, *"Give me lima beans!!"* It makes a difference, even as an adult, in your eating choices if you open up your refrigerator and see easy-to-grab healthy snacks or if you open up your pantry and see chips and candy. So, presence of healthy food, is a tried and true principle—what about the particulars?

I don't favor the French way of getting children to eat. This is probably one of the most unpopular things I could ever say, as it is very chic to try this seemingly exotic approach. In that it works, I believe it is because they carve out time to eat, provide quality food, and don't let children graze in between meals. A concern is that the other parts of it may create secondary undesirable behavior. When I think of the French way, in which children are told to wait (to the point of screaming) and then are force fed food, I can't help but think of the notorious service at French restaurants where customers are not tended to immediately and service is slow. Of course, I am sure not all French restaurants are like this, but I have to think that being forced to wait for food as children may cause such restauranteurs to expect others to wait for their food. This is just a hypothesis I have. I also have my doubts that French kids eat "everything." If the children are force fed French food, they grow up to like French food. This can shut down a curious approach to other foods and encourage instead snobbishness about their own food. This snobbishness is described in the book. A French woman describes American food as inferior, because, as she is quoted as saying, "Americans have no taste! Just compare a croissant to a doughnut!" (Le Billon, ch. 4). In this way, I think instead of "French Kids Like Everything," it may be, "French kids like French food," and to Americans their diet seems like "everything," because the food seems so exotic.

The "Division of Responsibility" worked really well for our family. My son (three years old at the time) had a problem with picky eating, which was causing health problems. He was drinking way too much milk and only wanted starchy items. This caused constipation, which caused bathroom accidents. The first day of trying a family style meal, I presented hardboiled eggs at our dining room table, as well as other items that he liked. He said, "I didn't want hardboiled eggs; I wanted scrambled eggs." I was astonished. No problem! Given our problem with getting him to eat anything but bread, I gladly made the scrambled eggs. He piled his plate up in a weird way with food on top of each other—not something I cared about whatsoever. He said while eating, "I love eating." That's exactly what I wanted to see. It was a major success! I am ashamed to admit that, before this, I had tried pressuring him into eating eggs, by denying him milk until he ate eggs, in what could have eventually made him hate eggs for the rest of his life, among other problems.

I'll be the first to tell you that making a family meal or snack, an "eating opportunity," as outlined in the Division of Responsibility, five or six times per day can be difficult to maintain. I did all right with it— until I had my third child, as well as some other very trying life events. When you are drowning in the demands of childcare and house chores; when you yourself don't get breakfast until noon, because you are dealing with the demands of small children all morning; when your infant won't stop crying; when your toddler won't stop whining; when you were up on and off all throughout the night; when making food that might just get wasted; when your kids are fighting you about sitting at the table—I find I sometimes just want to throw popcorn and Cheerios at them. I sometimes fantasize about having that French chef that is mandatory per government in France at every school in my own kitchen. But the virtues of family meals are many, and the investment may be worth it. Let me try to sell it to you with our experience with it.

I found this approach worked great with toddlers. There are some thinkers who say to offer children limited choices, such as asking, "Do you want scrambled eggs or hardboiled eggs?" I tried this, and it didn't really work. What if the child replies, "I want Cheerios!" The question can be too abstract for a young child. With a family style meal, they have many choices, much more than two, to choose from, and there is something about having the food out that helps. The food tantalizes them. They can watch other adults eating and enjoying the food. It is not an abstract question, as the food is right there, which works well for toddlers and preschoolers. I am reminded of the Montessori quote to zip your lips, say nothing, and model things for the child. If you did *Baby Led Weaning* (the book by Gill Rapley) when your child was an infant— where a child is not served jar food but instead goes straight to table food, which they feed to themselves—transitioning to family meals is seamless. The only differences are that the child eats from a plate, instead of a tray on a high chair. They can serve themselves (or have others help them) and they have more choice in what they want. In serving family style meals to toddlers, I found that I was much more likely to put a wider variety of food on their plate, because the food was simply there. Toddlers enjoy serving themselves, so this can serve as a great practical life activity. Throughout much of the toddler years, they are still adventurous eaters, so having a variety of food out may encourage them to try more foods. At some milestones, they seem to have a deep need to immerse themselves in sensory experiences, and playing with this may be fun, such as offering different flavored popsicles (you can make them homemade with real fruit!).

I find however that children become very picky by the time they are three years old. They enter milestones in their late twos in which they become very interested in right and wrong and insist on adhering to what is "right." Their senses seem to be much more sensitive and reactive to touch, smell, sound, etc. I don't ever want to cause you to underestimate your child, but you might expect "picky" eating in which they will not try something new starting around three years old, which lasts for several years.

With this method, no pressure at all should be put on the child to eat this or that, or anything at all. No praise or insults should be given about eating. Eating is a deeply personal thing. The only thing I say to my children is in response to their comments. If they say, "I love eating!" or "This food is so good," I smile and say, "It is so nice to enjoy our food!"

It is an act of love to eat with your children. The atmosphere that should be at the table should be one of comfortable presence, not pressure. Part of the power of this is that you sit with them to eat. They are much more likely to eat heartily with you sitting next to them. If my children don't come to the table, I say, "I would really enjoy your presence at the dinner table."

I found this style of serving food could be and was respectful for me as a parent too. I often don't eat lunch, because I am busy with the children. But if the rule is we all come to the table together, then I eat too. People sometimes see routines as restrictive, but this one is quite benevolent. I get to eat before I become starved, hormonal, and desperate for anything. When we go out, instead of grabbing fast food and eating it in the car, we bring food with us and make it a point to eat together, even if on the curb of a road while at a park. This wards off constant requests for milk or snacks while out.

It can be hard to get children to sit at the table, eat properly, and serve themselves properly. If you had time or patience previously to pressure them into eating something, why not convert all that energy into teaching table manners? From *French Kids Eat Everything*, "The children were simply not allowed to play with their food. Little fingers that dipped into bowls were kindly but firmly removed" (ch. 2). Investing in this may have pay off later, when you don't have to chase them around so that milk doesn't spill on the couch, or glasses get shattered on hard floors, and so on.

It is true, using the "Division of Responsibility," that meals are on a schedule, and food is not out at any time for the child to get, but I'd like to address just that. There are some books that say to have "healthy" snacks out for the children to pick whenever they want. I have grown to disagree with this. Hunger is a very complex issue. People eat for reasons beyond the fact that they are simply hungry. If they eat because the food simply looks good or is for comfort, then, when it is meal time, they aren't hungry. The book *Help Your Child with Extreme Picky Eating* advocates that it is important for the children to come to the table hungry, so they understand what this feels like. They then decide how much they eat, so they can learn what it feels like to be full. The authors argue that knowing to eat when hungry and stop when full is not automatic; it is a skill to develop. Getting them to come to the table is a lot easier if they are hungry. Almost every bit of nutrition advice says it is ideal for people to eat 5 or 6 times per day. Setting this routine for your children helps them learn this happy habit. For myself, I can tell you I lost a lot of weight by learning how many calories I should eat in one day and sticking to an eating schedule such that I ate that amount. If I strayed from this and started "grazing," which is what happens if you have snacks out, even if they are "healthy" ones, I would (and have) sabotaged my diet. I thus am now opposed to grazing, and I am especially opposed to people who leave junk food out for their kids to get at any time and then tell the child: "It's *your* job to manage your health and if you eat unhealthily, it's *your* fault for making poor decisions." No. Just no. Hormones are serious business and bad habits are hard to break. Healthy behavior needs to be taught and modeled in loving ways. This attitude and practice of "Cowboy up; figure it out on your own," while in a sea of toxic behavior, needs to stop.

One of the parenting battles I most dread is when other people pressure my children to eat—and from my many conversations with other parents, I am not alone in this battle. I especially dislike when someone makes a comment about my child or another child about their weight, such as they are too skinny. This should never, ever, be said, especially to the child. Saying it to a parent is also cruel and uncalled for. Telling children they are a "picky eaters" is also unhelpful. This is a label and lays the "problem" at the child's feet, sending the message that something is wrong with them, that this is the way they simply are, and that they can never and will never change. It is infuriating to me when people who have such obvious terrible eating habits and/or terrible relationships with food pressure my children to eat more, eat less, or lecture them on diet. This is not light banter. *This is verbal abuse.*

I also used to have trouble when I made dinner that other adults not in our immediate family would rush children to the table to eat immediately after I finished preparing dinner. Having just finished dinner, I am not necessarily ready to eat and therefore not at the table yet. Rushing children to the table without me doesn't work, because they need me, their mother, to sit with them. To prevent this, you might start each meal off with a special "signal" to initiate the meal. A family prayer or a toast are examples.

We make efforts to set boundaries and ask that people respect that our children can pick what and how much they want, but few can turn off their constant comments and hovering as the child eats. Still others judge parents who can't provide healthful enough food in their opinion. I will just add that providing meal after meal of healthful options, when a child rightfully might not eat any of it, is a difficult and challenging task. If people want to help, they could start by making healthy meals, sitting with the child in a loving and comfortable way, and modeling healthy eating habits *themselves*. Judgment, pressure, and insults are most unwelcomed and most harmful. Taking the advice to just zip your lips and demonstrate ideal behavior, rolling up your sleeves to help by cooking a healthy meal, being an example in your own food choices, being supportive, and being present *are* most helpful.

What is nice with this method is that parents have some control over parts of eating. It is nice to have some influence over the "when." This method resolved many problems for us. We used to have a problem with our first son being hungry late at night, having to come down to eat after bedtime. When I arranged it such that there was no snacking or grazing before dinner time, such that he came to dinner hungry, he ate much more heartily, and then went to bed at bedtime. I found my son ate a lot more with this method than he ever did before, when I would let snacks be out all day.

It is also nice to have some influence over "what" children eat, as is allowed in the Division of Responsibility diet approach for children.

This was necessary for us, as we had some problems with a diet causing medical problems. What to serve children is a source of much confusion and anxiety for many parents, and for good reason. What is healthy to serve children seems to be in a state of flux with much contradictory information over what sound nutrition is. Many nutritional problems exist, including obesity and digestive health problems. When I let go of all pressure tactics, I didn't want to influence the "what" to eat, except in obvious things like sugary snacks, until I got scientific advice over what a proper diet should be. From my reading, this is what I know. First, it is becoming increasingly clear that sugar and starch are the main problem in typical American diets. I have read many health books on this, including *The Insulin Resistance Diet* (Hart and Grossman) and *The Glycemic Load Diet* (Thompson). Sugar and starch do more than add calories; they cause a hormonal chain reaction in people predisposed to insulin problems, which although thoughts vary on how many people are predisposed, is a lot of people. If you gain weight in your belly, you are almost certainly prone to insulin problems, as outlined in *The Insulin Resistance Diet*.

It needs to be noted that the main problem in obesity is from diet and not lack of exercise. No amount of little legs pumping all over a soccer field can stop the effects of a poor diet. I keep my kids away from sugar as much as possible, not by demonizing it, but by simply not having it in my house.

For the digestive problems that arose from my son's past diet, I visited a pediatric urologist. To prevent constipation, they recommended limiting him to two glasses of milk per day; to limit rice, cheese, and bananas; and to increase other fruits and vegetables. I am unconvinced that this is enough to prevent constipation, a problem more present in American children than most would like to admit. I read a book about this problem specifically, *Cure Constipation Now*. The author, Dr. Wes Jones, prescribes that people need more *insoluble* fiber. He writes, "Contrary to just about everything you have ever read, fruits, vegetables, and even whole-wheat or whole-grain breads and pastas are generally not a reliable source of good, high-quality fiber for maintenance of healthy bowel habits" (ch. 2). Insoluble fiber is hard to get, unless your children are eating All-Bran for breakfast. Dr. Jones recommends a particular bread, Fiber Five, also sometimes called High Five Fiber Bread, as one that provides enough insoluble fiber, but it is not widely available. (Perhaps phone calls to your local grocery store could alleviate the lack of availability.) Some authors have recommended a small amount of prune juice for children to help with this problem. I found this is easier said than done. This lack of availability of insoluble fiber is one example of how the odds are stacked against American parents when it comes to providing a healthful diet. If bread was more like bread used to be over one hundred years ago, which was packed with insoluble fiber, this one change alone might take this otherwise starchy food item, which is unhealthful, and make it healthful. This food, bread, which children so reliably love, would be an engine for health; whereas now, it is an engine for diabetes and other diseases.

Sometimes parents worry about their children getting not enough protein. From the book *Helping Your Child with Extreme Picky Eating*, most children more than get their daily protein.

In the morning, sometimes, my son would get up before me and make his own breakfast. I have no problem with this. We are a hybrid of approaches here, but I do like the Division of Responsibility. My favorite part of it is how often my children tell me "I love eating" or "My food is delicious!" It is just great. This is exactly how food should be seen: as delicious fuel that happily satisfies hunger, not as a source of battles or frustration.

Toddler Conflict Resolution Tools

This is a list of the conflict resolution tools that I will discuss in Section Two, which outlines the cognitive milestones.

Distraction

If children don't want to do something, you can distract them with something pleasant. For instance, if you want to put a hat on a very young child, you might put the hat on and then distract them with a funny face and song until they forget the hat is on.

Redirection

If children are doing something harmful or you don't like, you can redirect them to an activity that satisfies their desire to learn but respects something valuable to you. If they are banging on something that might break, you might offer a sturdy toy to bang on.

Give a Choice Where Inaction is Not a Choice

If a child is being uncooperative, you give the child two choices of how to proceed but one of those choices is something where you will act on their behalf. An example is "You can get in the car seat on your own or I will put you in." If they don't get in, you follow through on your statement.

Give in Fantasy What Cannot be Given in Reality

When a toddler wants something wildly fantastic or impossible to give, this may help. If they ask you to hand the moon to them, you might say, "I really wish I could reach up, grab it and hand it right to you!"

Soothing

If children are in pain, they need soothed before asking them to behave better or giving them information about what to do next time.

"I" statements

If you have a problem with what the child is doing, you can state it with a three-part "I" statement which includes how you feel, what the action is, and why you don't like it. "I don't like when you kick my leg, because it hurts me."

Give Information

If a child is doing something improper, you reinforce positive behavior by pointing out what objects are used for instead of what not to do. "Chairs are for sitting. Trampolines are for jumping on."

Normalization

This is a concept presented by Montessori. If you can find an activity that the child loves to do over and over again, it can help increase the child's attention span and reduce overall number of meltdowns.

Emotion Coaching

During times of calm, you talk to the child about emotions and do activities to help them sort out their emotions for better emotional regulation when they are capable. Talking about a happy and sad part of the day at night is one example.

Design the Environment

Being mindful of the environment and designing it to reduce conflict. You might keep valuables up high or put a chain lock on the door, so they can't escape from the house.

Give a Lesson

In times of calm or sometimes even shortly after something happens, give a lesson on an ideal behavior. One wonderful way to do this is to take a real conflict that happened and act it out by either drawing it or creating a puppet show, illustrating a better way to handle something next time. A play starring your child!

Storytelling

After something scary happens, retell the story, slowly at first, so the child can process the event.

Routines

Setting up a routine for daily activities such as bedtime.

Section Two: Cognitive Milestones in the Toddler Years

Introduction to the Toddler Milestones

Milestone: A significant event or stage in the life, progress, development, or the like of a person, nation, or willful entity.

The following documents the cognitive milestones that my research found from 18 to 36 months, or 1½ to 3 years of age. Each milestone lists the times when irritable periods start, when they are at their most intense, and when they end. I sometimes round off the ages to the nearest week. This may cause a natural two- to three-day misalignment as you compare your child. Calculating the dates from your child's due date is more likely to be accurate, especially if your child was born premature. However, for full term children (born at 37 weeks or later), some parents report that a date in between the birth and due date works better if not the birth date itself.

At each milestone, I separate the abilities into distinctive and variable abilities. The distinctive abilities are central to the dominant new skill of the milestone. They are highly characteristic of the milestone. When you read them, you will see a pattern in each that led to the milestone being named what it is. The variable abilities are skills that tend to vary from child to child much more. The skills assigned to the variable category are typically academic skills like counting or reading. Not all milestones have a variable section. I list the earliest a parent has ever seen their child show any skill. This is so you know when the earliest that it may be possible to develop this skill. However, for many children, any given skill but especially the variable skills are likely to be seen at older ages.

Please do not compare your child negatively against this list of skills. The research data reflect the observations of many parents and they pick the earliest date reported (not the average or the mean) for seeing a specific behavior. It is statistically next to impossible that any child—your child— will hit all developmental milestones at their earliest possible. I encourage you, therefore, to focus on the skills you do see and nurture them. Most children who are "behind" will eventually catch up and do just fine. If you are worried that a child is "behind," many of the activities listed at each milestone can help develop budding and appropriate skills.

Please also do not swallow the milestones whole. There are a lot of them and there will surely be trying times, but please don't inhale the totality of it all at once. They won't happen all at once: They happen over the course of 18 months. Please take each one at a time. I assure you that you can handle them!

Conflict resolution ideas are included with each milestone, but the list is not exclusive to all approaches that may work. If you have found something that works for you, please don't feel that what you are doing is wrong just because I did not list it. I occasionally identify why some tools do not work at a certain age, given where the child is at cognitively, such as why asking children who have not hit the milestone of "Decision Making" to make a decision probably won't work. However, within a certain framework, I do not see any approach as "wrong." The paradigm that I work within is the medical paradigm, "Above all else, do no harm." Otherwise, if someone has found an approach that works with children, I always give it its due to find out more about it and when and how it would best apply. Please see the conflict resolution ideas as options, not as commandments.

One of the best things you can do as a parent is find another parent who has a child or children the exact same age as your child. All of this is so age-related. It is very helpful to swap stories about sleep troubles and behavioral difficulties. Perhaps this book can help as you wade through these issues. I offer free printouts with a chart and summary with highlights for each milestone at my website, www.TheObservantMom.com. I invite you to join the Facebook forum about this book series, "Misbehavior is Growth—The Discussion," to connect with other parents. My goal is to unleash people's creativity and to develop highly robust tools to deal with these rocky developmental cycles.

Activity ideas are provided for each milestone, but not all children may be interested in them. If a child is not interested in an activity, please put it away for another day. Also, please don't feel the need to do all activities. Do the ones that work for your child, your time, your level of interest and patience, and your financial situation. Many of the activities can be done using materials other than the ones described and with materials you might already have. Everything listed is simply an example to illustrate a type of activity you might do. Your local library may have some or similar materials for you to use.

The activity recommendations provided are not all-inclusive, because ideas for new activities are endless and constantly being invented. It is one of my greatest joys to discover where my children are cognitively, along with what their interests are, and come up with a creative activity that may delight them. Other activities not listed may also delight your child. This is where *you* come in. Each family will invest in cognitive growth in its own unique way. Every family is made up of parents and children who have their own unique interests and skill sets. I talk to some mothers who tell me they love to talk, and they see how well their children communicate because of it. Other parents routinely expose their children to live music. Personally, I am an introvert who can't sing a note, and I focused on many science and math activities with my children. Your unique talents bring a lot to the table, but must be reconciled with your child's natural interests, which might vary from yours. My daughter is an extrovert whose passion is singing. I do everything in my power to nurture this despite my lack of singing ability.

I hope that this information, which is intended to clarify your toddler's mental growth, helps you to devise creative activities for your unique child!

Toddler Milestone 1 – Language Comprehension

Starts: 18 months
Most Intense: 18 months, 1 week
Ends: 19 Months
Irritable Period Summary

Clingy

Occasional Meltdowns

Sleep schedule becomes erratic, e.g., unreliable nap times

Most Intense Period

Very clingy with many meltdowns

New Abilities Summary

Distinctive

Explosion in language comprehension

Understands and executes the function of an object based solely on a verbal clue, e.g., gets a jacket after the word "jacket" is said

More respectful of others, e.g., doesn't step on their sibling

Says more words, about one new word per day

More awareness of and interest in body parts

Variable

Can follow a sequence where there are two events, e.g., wipes up a mess and then throws the paper towel in the garbage

Talks in complete sentences (three or four words)

Understands the idea of counting and may be counting

Many fine motor skills

Irritable Period Description

I didn't notice this irritable period with my first-born son. He was, however, in a Montessori school at the time, and I didn't notice irritable periods as well. But at around 18 months, I noticed that my daughter (my second child) wanted to be held a lot and occasionally had an intense meltdown. At 18 months, 1 week, it was at its most intense. I noticed fussiness, though less intense, on and off after this for about one month. Her nap schedule kept jumping around, ranging from being sleepy from as early as around 11:30 am to as late as 2:00 pm.

New Abilities Description

The first skill I noticed was that my daughter was starting to understand more words. "[T]here is an impressive increase in verbal language comprehension around 18 months" (van de Rijt and Plooij, ch. 12). I was surprised when I asked my son to get his jacket, and my daughter ran over to get hers. This showed that she knew what "jacket" meant, based on the verbal clue alone and, also, that she understood its use. Other mothers report that their child can follow through on a sequence of events, such as getting dog food out and then putting it in a bowl.

What I really noticed was how well my daughter started to enunciate words. Up until this milestone, she understood many words, but now she was *saying* many and with clarity—seemingly a new word or two every day! Other mothers report their children speaking in full sentences. Yet others don't see any language explosion just yet. It seems the potential for language development starts at this age but is highly dependent on other factors.

Other interests noticed were doing fine motor activities, such as scribbling. My daughter copied many things that her brother and I did, such as putting rubber bands on a Geoboard (a mathematical manipulative with a grid made of pegs that rubber bands can be stretched around).

Touchpoints—Birth to Three describes a study done by psychologist Michael Lewis (in *Developmental Disabilities: Theory, Assessment, and Intervention*) in which 18-month-old children could, if rouge was put on their noses and shown a mirror, move to wipe it off their own nose. This is as opposed to previous ages (15 months) in which they tried to wipe the rouge as seen in the reflection of the mirror. Dr. Brazelton describes this as an "astonishing new leap in self-awareness." He follows up this study with this thought about children exploring the distinct parts of their body:

> Not surprisingly, then, self-exploration at this age becomes heightened. A toddler is intrigued with her eyes, her nose, her mouth. When she gets a chance, she is intrigued with her navel and her genitalia. (ch. 11)

Feedback

Hailey has a better enunciation of words. She is able to count from 1 to 6, and she knows the difference between night and day. – Christina

Super helpful confirming my suspicion of a [cognitive milestone] now at 18 months. – Jennifer

[W]e just ended the [milestone] starting around 18 Months. My daughter had night-waking, early waking, and a shorter afternoon nap. She ate less (she's got all of her teeth so it is unrelated to teething). After it ended (about 3 weeks long), she had an explosion in vocabulary and pronounces things much more clearly. She now repeats back everything I say and can say a few sentences! She is now capable of learning a new word after only hearing it once. She is now super happy and busy! She also weaned on her own after this [milestone], easily, with no tears. She seems very independent and happy at the moment. – Lacey Quintero

[S]he would follow through with some sequences at 18 months [...] something would spill, she would take a paper towel, clean it up, and throw it in the trash can. Some sequences, I noticed closer to that 20 months, like scooping out the dog food from the container, and putting it in each dog's bowl. – Lacey Quintero

Conflict Resolution

Authors in the *Positive Discipline* series recommend just acting in order to get a toddler to cooperate with you. From *Positive Discipline: A – Z*:

Another variation on the "decide what you will do" method of parenting is acting instead of talking. Listen to yourself for one day. You might be amazed how many useless words you say. Or listen to parents bargaining with their kids at the grocery store, begging them at the department store, nagging them at the park, and explaining endlessly to them when it's time to move from point A to point B. Over 75 percent of the problems parents have with young children would probably disappear if parents talked less and acted more. Children tune parents out because parents talk too much. [...] It is perfectly okay to take children by the hand and start walking, or lift them up and carry them to bed, or set them in the tub when they are having a fit about taking a bath. It is disrespectful to yell, nag, lecture, beg, order, and threaten. Give up counting to three; just zip your lips and act. You'll be amazed at the results. (Nelsen, Lott and Glenn, Part 1)

Throughout the toddler years, it is always acceptable to just act. But it's certainly nicer if the child is calm and cooperative. What makes my approach slightly different than what was just quoted is that I actively seek to calm my child down. I invest a lot in empathy.

I found it was unrealistic to offer a child at this age limited choices or get them involved in decision making. For instance, let's say you need them to get a shirt on. A parent might try to offer two shirts and let the child pick one. My experience is that when you offer two shirts, the child might pick one, but the more common answer was "Chase me." I found they were like the character Dory from *Finding Nemo*: they could not hold on to a thought for terribly long. At this age (and younger), the tools of distraction and redirection work better for a child.

Distraction is doing something to shift a child's mind to a different focus so that a task which they are resistant to can be accomplished. If children won't put their shirt on, you can, for instance, sing their favorite song which distracts them from not wanting to put the shirt on. You then put the shirt on while they are enthralled with the song you are singing. You can distract them with anything whatsoever—whatever happens to catch their attention. The issue for them probably has nothing to do with the shirt. That they don't hold on to a thought for long makes distraction work, but it also makes offering limited choice not work. Giving choices works better after the child reaches Toddler Milestone 6, Decision Making (2 years, 2 months).

The other tool is that of redirection. If children are doing something that you find unacceptable, you can find a similar activity that you do find acceptable. For example, if a child is hitting, pick them up and move them and maybe let them high five you. If they are knocking over cups and plates, give them wood blocks to knock over or something similar that you are comfortable with.

The use and value of redirection and distraction as parenting tools are outlined in the book *Positive Discipline: The First Three Years*:

> Until children reach the age of reason, which starts around age three (and is an ongoing process that even some adults have not fully mastered), supervision and distraction are the most effective parenting tools. (Nelsen, Erwin and Duffy, ch. 1)

Some moms report that their child would respond to verbal requests. I did find my children were more responsive to requests such as "Please don't step on your brother," but I found I still often needed to use gentle hands-on methods to get my child to start or stop doing things. How many children you have and how many issues you have likely affects if you can rely on verbal requests alone or if you need to be hands on.

Activities

    Picture books to build vocabulary

    Montessori knobbed cylinders

    Sorting objects by color

    Knobbed puzzles

    Play-Doh (make little balls and snakes)

    Pencils for scribbling

    Provide a mirror

Picture Books

A great activity when they are entering a language explosion is to build the child's vocabulary with picture books. There are many picture books on the market which feature clear pictures of a variety of objects usually with the word printed next to the picture. An example is *First 100 Words* by Roger Priddy. I like to have at least one general picture book and one of just animals. You can expand this by getting books that feature one type of object, such as a picture book of flowers or whatever else is important to you for your child to learn. You can do body parts by simply pointing to you or your child's body parts.

There is an art to presenting new words. I used the three stages of learning as presented by Maria Montessori. The first stage is for instance simply pointing to a picture of a horse and say "horse." Stay at this stage for at least one day. You can point to as many pictures as you like. Simply enjoy the picture book and tell your child what the pictures are without asking any questions of the child.

Stage two is asking the child "Which one is the horse?" For this, I first use stage one by pointing, in this example, to the horse, and then immediately after this, I ask "Which one is the horse?" If the child cannot answer, you might try another picture, but for the exercise related to the horse, go back to stage one and don't ask what it is again until the next day. If they do answer correctly, you might ask what other pictures are, stopping when they seem to tire of the activity. This question at stage two is easy on purpose. It is also essential to learning as a person needs to use information for it to "stick." Humans learn well by touching things, and I found that if the child touched the picture of the horse after being asked to find it, it was as if the idea of "horse" were being downloaded into their brain.

Stage three is to point to a picture and ask, "What is this?" They then respond with "horse." If they can't answer, return to a previous stage and try again the next day. As they say "horse," they are practicing enunciation as well.

I often jumped around in stages when reading with my children, perhaps going to stage three with pictures they were comfortable with and scaling back to stage one with others they weren't comfortable with during the same reading session. At all times if I went further or scaled back was dependent on their answers and enthusiasm. Once they reach the third level of knowledge, they have mastered the idea.

Knobbed Cylinders

Knobbed cylinders are a great activity at this milestone (in fact even younger, but still very applicable now). Knobbed cylinders provide a strong control of error: the cylinder won't go in the block unless it's the right one. If a smaller cylinder goes into a wide hole, at the end of the activity, the child is left with too many cylinders, and they have an interesting puzzle to solve.

Do not step in and do this activity for them or correct them. The idea of this is they work through a challenge. This activity is in great alignment with where the child is at cognitively. At this age, they need gentle redirection and strong physical boundaries to help guide them the right way. These knobbed cylinders, which provide such a rigid structure yet a fun challenge, are perfect. It also helps develop fine motor skills for later activities.

These cylinders typically come in a set of four which change in the following ways: height, width, height and width, and height and width inversely. The easiest set to start with are the ones that change in width only. The next easiest are the ones that change in height and width (size). The next easiest are the ones that change in height only. I did not like the ones that change inversely where height decreased while width increased. I tried it myself and found it frustrating, not challenging, but you might have a different experience. My children never did these especially well even at the age of three when it continued to seem to be more of a guessing game to get the cylinders in than something that brought clarity to discerning height, width, and size, which is what the cylinders are meant to do.

These knobbed cylinders are currently rather expensive, as they are made of wood. I wonder if a manufacturer made them from plastic whether the cost would be greatly driven down, becoming more available to people. There are also wood cylinder sets that have only five cylinders per block. I think the educational value of these are just as good, and they are significantly less expensive.

Sorting Colors

To present colors to a child, find objects that are identical in all ways except color, such as Unifix Cubes and have the child simply sort the objects by color into piles. This warms up their mind to "seeing" what you are about to explain. After they have sorted the colors correctly, simply say "Red, Red," showing how the two they put together matched. This is, as previously described, the first stage of learning.

To really get an idea, I like to have two different materials explain the same concept. Perhaps have another object, such as colored golf tees, to again teach the idea the next day. Eventually move on to the other two stages of learning where you ask "Which is red?" (stage two) and finally "What is this?" (stage three).

I found presenting three colors at once worked best. I started with strongly contrasting colors at first such as red, yellow, and blue. Then I used red, orange, yellow. Then green, blue, purple. Then black, brown, white.

I found at this milestone, a child might only understand 1 or 2 colors. Developing the rest of the colors takes time and might not develop for another 2 or 3 months. It is normal to confuse orange and yellow or green and blue. Don't correct them. Just go back to sorting activities. If they don't like the activity, put it away for another day. I found sometimes my children would become uninterested in an activity because it was too easy for them. If you suspect this, jump to a later stage of learning and see how they do.

Toddler Milestone 2 – Strings Objects/Events Together

Starts: 19 Months, 3 Weeks
Most Intense: 20 Months
Ends: Shortly after 20 Months
Irritable Period Summary

Sleep problems

Extra crankiness

Wants to be held and put down over and over

Wants a lovey to go places with them

Most Intense Period

All of the above but more intense

New Abilities Summary

Distinctive

Follows along with simple, dramatic stories, in which events change, such as *We're Going on a Bear Hunt* by Helen Oxenbury and Michael Rosen

Loves songs with a twist, such as "Pop Goes the Weasel"

Arranges objects as to represent something real, e.g., Mr. Potato Head

Follows simple instructions

Says many words, mostly nouns and verbs

Variable

Builds more things

Know 1 or 2 colors

Understands the idea of counting and may be counting

Tries to sing part of song

Irritable Period Description

At one week shy of 20 months old, an irritable period starts. It's a doozy. My daughter wanted to be held non-stop. Then she couldn't decide if she wanted to be up or down. At 20 months on the dot, the irritable period was quite intense. I noticed this with my first child too.

It seemed impossible that another irritable period would occur so soon after the last one. I was admittedly in denial at first, but once I embraced it, it became easier to handle. I cancelled plans for one entire week just to be with my daughter. And it was worth it! She loved to be near me and had a look of, "Mommy, you're the best," while we sat together. My daughter grew a strong attachment to her blanket. She wanted to bring it everywhere. She found her first real lovey. She would very sweetly ask me to pick her up. However, I admit it can be frustrating when children can't decide if they want to be picked up or put down or when you are cooking every meal with a toddler on your hip.

We continued to notice after 20 months some crankiness. She could not tolerate missing nap time, which would cause her to be very cranky. I often played nursery rhymes just to calm her down. Several times, she woke up during the night. We noticed similar sleep problems with my son.

New Abilities Description

I noticed my daughter started to love drama. At the 18-month milestone, I strongly recommend simple picture books, which are used primarily to build their vocabulary. At this milestone, less than 2 months later, I would recommend short, simple stories. My daughter for instance loved *We're Going on a Bear Hunt* by Helen Oxenbury and Michael Rosen. The family goes looking for a bear then "*Oh my goodness, they find a bear!!*" My daughter would scream with delight. In this way, she could follow along with the events of the book, which were different but all related and, assembled, told one story.

Songs with interesting or whacky twists which switched from one theme to another, e.g., quiet to loud, were also fun. An example is the song "Pop Goes the Weasel." It starts out melodic and then "POP!" goes the weasel. Another fun one may be "Ring Around the Rosie" where children dance in a circle and then fall down.

My daughter could say "ya" and mean it now. She said two words together, typically a noun and a verb. She once spilled milk, got a paper towel, cleaned it up, and threw the paper towel away. She executed these two related events in a row, though other mothers report seeing this at an earlier milestone.

When my daughter scribbled, she would say she made something, such as Mommy or a race car. My son also started to build things. He once put green Mega Bloks together and said they were an alligator. My daughter could assemble Mr. Potato Head's face correctly. Both children loved Mega Bloks (large-sized plastic "bricks" that can be connected with pegs into slots) and LEGO DUPLO toys (large-sized plastic pieces that fit together to make specific objects or people). In this way, they put together disparate parts and can see the "whole" better.

My daughter showed she knew a few colors and could start to count. Other mothers report seeing their children count at the previous milestone. I include the difference in when this is seen to emphasize that children develop at their own pace.

Feedback

Hailey can now count to 10, she can say her ABC's, and is able to string 2 words together now for sentences. – Christina

Confirming [Toddler Milestone 2]. My 19 month old (due date July 13 2015) has been clinging to her puppy lovey, wanting to take him everywhere; not eating as much, a few sleep issues, clingy, crying some at daycare where she never did before. – Rachel Malone

My son is currently in [Toddler Milestone 2]. He is not sleeping well, is cranky and carries his giraffe (lovey) everywhere! At the same time his vocabulary has exploded. – Sarah Lewis

I am happy to report that the "[milestone 2] storm" has ended. THANK GOODNESS! My daughter is 20 months, plus 5 days and has miraculously returned to easy bedtimes at 6:45 PM, no night wakings, and sleeping in until 7:30 AM, no more clinging, no more tantrums, and is just being easier/happier in general. The worst part was DEFINITELY exactly at 20 months, as you indicated. We survived!!!! — Lacey Quintero

Conflict Resolution

A most welcomed advancement was an ability to follow simple instructions more reliably. When my daughter was using a marker where she shouldn't, I could ask her, "Can you do that on the white board?" And she did. I no longer had to physically move her as much.

Activities

Simple dramatic stories

Silly songs

Count stairs as you go up them

Building things, e.g., Mega Bloks or Mr. Potato Head

Continue sorting objects by color

Counting Stairs

Counting stairs as you walk up them is the best counting activity you can do. Given their greater persistence of thought, I recommend it at this milestone. Counting stairs as you go up them is a very "hands-on" activity, but of course with the child's feet. There is natural 1:1 correspondence as you go up each stair. The child can naturally see that numbers get higher as you count higher and as you go higher on the stairs. It also takes no additional time or resources than what you already use as you go up the stairs.

Counting Pegs on Mega Bloks

One activity that seemed to help counting was Mega Bloks. I include this activity to show that you may already have a common toy (Mega Bloks) in your house that can act as math manipulatives without having to buy anything specially designed and expensive. One of the Mega Blok pieces is a row of four. My son, on his own, would put four single Mega Bloks on this long row of four. As he did it, he would count. The row of four allowed him to perceptually understand what "4" was. After this, he reliably could count up to 4 or 5.

Songs

These songs may be loved by the child. Many of them have actions and motions that can be used in addition:

Yankee Doodle

Pop Goes the Weasel

Ring Around the Rosie

Spiderman (theme song)

Slippery Fish

Bringing Home a Baby Bumblebee

Alphabet Song

Twinkle Twinkle Little Star

Wheels on the Bus

Tiny Turtle

Hush Little Baby

Happy and You Know It

Toddler Milestone 3 – Symbolic Thought

Starts: 21 Months, 1 Week
Most Intense: 21 months, 3 weeks
Ends: 22 months
Irritable Period Summary

Clingy at first, asks to be held a lot

Wants only their primary caregiver

Stalls at nap and bedtime, becomes demanding of primary caregiver's time

Picky, e.g., about what clothes to wear or other similar issue

Wants a lovey

Most Intense Period

Demanding, picky, may hit or throw, separation anxiety

New Abilities Summary

Distinctive

Understands abstract symbols, such as letters, better

Concrete to abstract matching games become possible, such as matching a Cinderella doll to a picture of Cinderella

More complete sentences

Simple conversational flow in how they speak

Responsive to questions

Understands difference in gender

Variable

Practical life activities explode: turning lights on and off, buckling seat belts and such

Capable of learning many colors

Counting becomes refined

Irritable Period Description

At 21 months, 1 week, my daughter became very clingy. She wanted to be held a lot. She only wanted mommy. She started to demand more and more around nap time (story after story, song after song), before being put down to bed. She became picky about what clothes to wear. Perhaps now that she could identify the attribute of an object better, she wanted a particular shirt, e.g., the one with sparkles on it. She

115

wanted to take her blanket everywhere. This behavior, of being demanding and picky, got to be at its worst around 21 months, 3 weeks and then dissipated.

New Abilities Description

At this milestone, a child really explodes in doing what Montessori called practical life activities. My daughter wanted to buckle seat belts, turn light switches on and off, and help me make food. A little stool that helps a child to reach things is a great "toy" for this age, though make sure to baby-proof higher counters well. My daughter pushed her stool around often and loved it.

Towards the end of this milestone, my daughter showed a strong understanding of all colors and she started to learn most letters. She could take a concrete object, such as a doll, and match it to its drawn representation, showing she understood abstract, symbolic pictures better.

My daughter started to say complete sentences at this time. Her first sentence was, "I kissed Mommy." This ability may have been a product of the last milestone; it's hard to say—and other moms report their children speak in complete sentences at earlier milestones. She also started to develop a conversational flow to how she talked. I first noticed this when I said, "Where is your pillow?" and she said, "I'll find it!" At a younger age, she may have said she "found" something, but now she answered a question.

She also showed she knew differences in gender. She showed this by pointing to any male and saying "daddy," and any female and saying "mommy."

Dr. Brazelton describes in *Touchpoints—Birth to Three* that by the two-year checkup, a child is able to know a difference in gender. This means that sometime between the 18-month checkup and two-year checkup that a pediatrician typically sees a child, they developed this ability:

> Gender identification - A boy may have already absorbed his father's behavior and a girl, her mother's. This identification is often clear by two years of age and speaks to the power of imitation and early awareness of a child's own gender. (ch. 12)

Dr. Brazelton also describes how at the two-year checkup, the child is capable of "symbolic play."

Feedback

Hailey's communication has grown tremendously. I was able to tell her to go to her room and find her socks, and she was able to follow through. She came back to the living room and said, "I found the socks!" – Christina

21 month [milestone 3] here. Suddenly wants to be held and carried by mom (me) most of the time. Asks me to go with him wherever he goes. – Dinára Saparóva

Was just wondering if my son is going through a [cognitive milestone]. And yup! […] 21m and 1 week exactly. The hardest we have ever gone through. We are both exhausted. – Safa Inoon

Confirming the Toddler milestone 3 (9 days shy of 22 months when adjusted to due date). The last 3 days have been the "stormy" meltdown city! Today, I actually had to stop myself from laughing because my daughter had an epic meltdown when I told her she could not drive my car to the store because she was too little. She was trying to open the passenger door and it was just such a sincere emotional meltdown and the ridiculous nature of this meltdown just made me laugh (don't worry she didn't hear or see me laughing). [...] I've had crayons thrown at my face twice today (totally out of character for her). She is exhibiting separation anxiety from our DOGS and cries every time they have to go outside. She's having epic meltdowns about every hour, usually over nothing. Whew! We are probably towards the end of this now, and the beginning wasn't bad at all. This must be the worst of it. – Lacey Quintero

I noticed some new language skills today! My daughter has been repeating words/phrases/short sentences for a while, but today she came up with two on her own. Dad asked "where's Mom?" And she said "Mom making eggs," which was actually true. – Lacey Quintero

During breakfast she also said "more ham pieces please" after she had picked out all of the ham pieces out of her scrambled eggs. She also pointed out the letter "P" on my husband's t-shirt without prompting and I saw her tracing letters from a word on her placemat with her fork. – Lacey Quintero

When adjusted for due date, today should be 22 months for us. This week we noticed the "picky clothes" issue crop up for the first time. My daughter literally sobs over her "rainbow shirt" once she has to throw it in the hamper and change into PJ's. The next morning when I'm getting her dressed, and most days lately, she looks down at her shirt and starts crying and pulling at it, sobbing "rainbow shirt." Also, her conversational skills definitely improved (very responsive to questions). She continues to refine her sentences and speak new ones. She's started to be a bit bossy, saying things to me like "Mommy sit down." And telling the dog to do things too. She is singing songs, but only picks up certain words/phrases from the songs, and can't quite sing the whole songs yet. – Lacey Quintero

Conflict Resolution

This irritable period wasn't terrible for us, but it again caught me off guard. And there is something about this particular milestone that really now defines the child as a "Toddler." Maybe it is how picky and demanding they can be or how they can't make up their mind about what they want. The pickiness is new and was originally difficult for me to handle. After two children and much reading, I found that an effective way to deal with children who are picky about clothing is, as described in previous milestone descriptions, to distract them. Put a blanket on your head to make them laugh, sing a song, whatever it is—you know your child best. Offering a choice of what to wear or waiting for them to make up their mind is still unrealistic. I found my children were never happy with any choice. Distraction *worked*.

It is acceptable to just pick up children and have them do what you ask, such as get in the bathtub or car seat. I recommend distraction though, because it's still easier to pick up a child who is calm and cooperative than one who is fighting you.

Activities

Use a step-stool to reach light switches and counters

Match concrete objects to abstract symbols

Letter puzzle

Teach adjectives

Present starkly different objects to teach words

Concrete to Abstract Matching Games

A great activity is to match a concrete object a drawing of that object. An example of this is to match a Cinderella doll to a picture of Cinderella. This is an important pre-reading activity. You show the child that the symbols and pictures in books *mean* something You can make many activities like this for teaching purposes as well, such as matching different model airplanes to their picture in a book, which helps the child to differentiate the types of airplanes.

To do this in a way that the concrete object and drawing are exact, you can take a knobbed shape puzzle, which has puzzle pieces of a square, oval, etc., and then trace the puzzle pieces on a piece of paper. It will be easier for the child if you color these shapes in. The child then, for instance, places the square puzzle piece on the square on the paper. These activities are what Maria Montessori called moving from concrete to abstract.

This is an example of a concrete to abstract activity. I like to do this one to teach my children what shoe what goes on what foot. Trace the child's foot and then match the proper shoe to what you traced. This shows them that what shoe goes on what foot is based on the shape of the foot. Don't be surprised if they purposely match the shoes to the wrong feet!

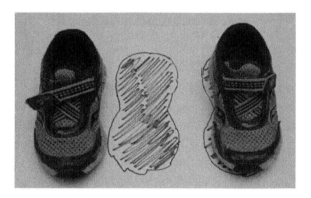

Letter Puzzle

To teach letters, I used a simple wooden letter puzzle and the three stages of learning. The puzzle is nice as there is a strong physical boundary and the child must orient the letter correctly. I did this coinciding with or after doing other concrete to abstract activities (e.g., a Cinderella doll to her drawn picture.) I found teaching letters was different than teaching words. A letter is an abstract symbol as opposed to an object like "horse." I found that the concrete to abstract activities helped to teach letters.

I taught letter names first, not sounds, which is different than is done in The Montessori Method. I found it too awkward to try to teach sounds initially. I also did it this way because the child can better learn letters by singing the Alphabet Song after completing the puzzle. The

Alphabet Song acts as the control of error as they point to letters and sing, "A, B, C, D ..."

I taught letter sounds later, and my children didn't have a problem grasping that a letter was named something but "said" something different when used to read. Children know a cow is a "cow" but says "moo" and similarly they can understand A is "A" and "says" "ahh."

I also did not worry about whether I taught lower or upper-case letters first. It is true that most letters in books are lower case. However, some of the first words they might be interested in are typically in all upper-case letters, such as how the word "POP!" might be found on a page in a book. I found that at the milestone of Memory Expansion a child can retain all lower and upper-case letters and their sounds.

I also liked to match movable letters to large images of letters in a book. This facilitates drawing children in to the book and gives relevance to the letters they see.

Teaching Adjectives

You can possibly work on the idea of possessives at this milestone. For instance, point to a picture of a cow and say, "The *cow's* nose," then to a picture of a pig and say, "The *pig's* nose."

Starkly Contrasting Objects to Teach Words

Teaching more abstract concepts (adjectives) directly is an ideal activity starting at this milestone. After for instance they do the short/tall cylinders, grab the shortest and tallest cylinder. Simply point to one and say "short." Point to the other and say "tall." Then proceed with the three stages of learning as described in the chapter on teaching.

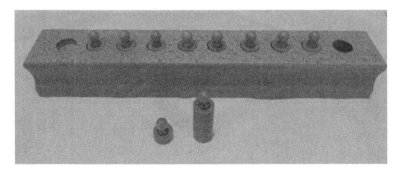

I did but one lesson like this with my son, and three weeks later, he pointed to a small and tall tree and said, "That tree is short! That tree is tall!" Montessori describes how children start making spontaneous observations of the environment like this after they learn the exact concept.

Think of as many words as you can teach by pointing to them and giving the word to your toddler. I tried to teach any word I could think of. Some examples: tie a string to a toy to teach the word "hanging" or drop a dense object in the bathtub to teach "sink."

Toddler Milestone 4 – Memory Expansion

Starts: 22 Months, 3 weeks
Most Intense: 23 months
Ends: 23 months, 3 weeks
Irritable Period Summary

Starts out with a child who is simply clingy

Defiant in doing normal routines, especially going to sleep

Cries

Skips naps

Wants only their primary caregiver at certain times

Demanding of time

Most Intense Period

Cries easily, wants to be held, refuses naps, demands large amount of time from primary caregiver

New Abilities Summary

Distinctive

Learns many words rapidly in a short amount of time

Increase in memory, such as singing almost an entire song

Remembers an answer to a question, such as what color something is, without seeing it

Persists at activities that are more open-ended and require visual discrimination, such as putting a train track set together

Variable

Initiates conversations

States opinions

Uses more complex sentences, with subjects, objects, verbs, and adjectives

Re-enacts simple stories

Much more delicate fine motor control, e.g., careful in handling and transferring objects

Better at puzzles, knobbed cylinders

Irritable Period Description

At about 1 week shy of 23 months, I noticed one morning that my daughter literally clung to my shirt. She also became more defiant and resistant to doing normal routines, like being put in the crib for naptime. At 23 months on the dot, from the due date for us, it was intense. My daughter was fine—until she wasn't. She cried easily and wanted to be held. She demanded I stay with her for about 45-60 minutes before naptime, lest she scream intensely after I left. She sometimes skipped naps.

New Abilities Description

The first thing I noticed about this milestone is a larger intensity. My daughter could complete an entire letter puzzle. She had almost the entire Alphabet Song memorized and could sing it. She could answer questions like, "What color is Thomas [from Thomas the Train]?" without seeing a picture or toy figure of Thomas in front of her. She once re-enacted a scene from Thomas the Train using two toy trains. She could do The Memory Game, which was an app on the iPad.

She was also more forward about her opinions and starting conversations. She said "That's crazy!" about something once—a statement of opinion.

She said to me, "Mommy, it's nice to see you," once. In the last milestones, she started to say complete sentences and responded to questions. Now she was initiating conversations. Her sentences became more complex. "I want more juice." This is a sentence with a subject, verb, object, and adjective. Before she may have said simply "more" or "more juice."

Dr. Brazelton describes the typical language development that he sees of 2-year-old children at their checkup, "A two-year-old will be using verbs to make short sentences and is beginning to use simple adjectives. 'Go to store.' 'Pretty dress.' 'I want that. It's nice.'"

My daughter took an interest in cutting with scissors. This is a more complicated activity than other fine motor activities. She also took a strong interest in transferring objects from one container to the next, like serving herself eggs from a pan. As the milestone went on, whereas before she may have dumped a bag of cheese or Cheerios while attempting to serve herself, she became very careful about serving herself. She could reach in, get a handful of Cheerios, and carefully transfer them to her other hand. Dr. Brazelton describes the fine motor skills of two-year-old children after observing them with a particular toy set:

The child might then bring the wind-up truck to the 'house.' Placing the dolls delicately on the truck, he will line them up flat, parallel with the floor, so as not to drop them out. He then winds the key to make the truck run. The level of delicacy with which a child handles toys, his fine motor competence as he winds a key, for instance, tells me that that aspect of his neuro-motor system is intact. (ch. 12)

My daughter persisted at activities such as putting a toy train track set together. This is something that doesn't have as much of a rigid structure to guide the child, such as the knobbed cylinders do, but must be put together by the judgment of their eye.

Feedback

She is able to recall things from past events. We went to a birthday party recently and she saw birthday presents. I explained to her what birthdays meant. A few days later I was wrapping Christmas presents and she says to me, "Happy birthday to me!" – Christina

Oh dear... confirming [milestone 4], bang on 23mth from due date and wow... just wow. – Britney Baldwin

Today my husband said, "Luke must be in cognitive milestone]! He's awful!" I looked at the [research posted], and sure enough [milestone 4] appears to be near. Thankful for this info - it gives purpose to the crazy and reassures me that it's temporary! – Rebecca Schreiber

[Milestone 4] is brutal! My son is about 23.5 months old (going by due date), and he is driving me crazy! He is becoming so much more verbal, but the whining, the tantrums, the clingy behavior...ugh. And he's barely eating and wanting to nurse constantly. I can't wait to put this one behind us. – Nicole Kiel

Toddler Milestone 4: we are right at 23 months and my daughter is super clingy with me only. She has to join me every time I use be bathroom, she is refusing to eat unless she is sitting in my lap and I am feeding her. She knows how to use a fork but has stopped doing it during this time. Also, she has been crawling around like a baby! When she is in her car seat, she has started to scream "Mommy" repeatedly for the entire drive. Her one nap of the day has gone down from her usual hour to only 30 minutes. She is constantly complaining that things are "missing" even though they are just out of sight. For example, the dog is missing if he's in the next room, the blanket is missing if it's on the floor, Mom is missing if she's in the kitchen, and the house is missing if we are in the car. As far as skills go, she is just now starting to sing songs but usually can only get phrases right in the song. She woke up this morning counting to 3, whereas before she could only repeat the numbers after I said them. – Lacey Quintero

Whoa we are still in the intense whining part of this milestone. It's been rough for a few days, with constant crying and whining. One of the big things I've noticed is that she is also talking less. In instances where she normally would have answered me in a sentence form, she is now just making this weird sound/noise instead. I can't really describe the noise, but thought I'd mention it because my friend's son made the exact same noise repeatedly (and also stopped talking during that time) right at 23 months. I remember thinking how strange it was, but now I see my daughter doing the same thing. She has barely touched her food this week. I'm lucky to get one good meal in her per day. I cannot believe how much she's crawling around. If I wasn't aware of these phases, this would have really worried me with all the "regressive" behavior. I can't wait for it to be OVER! – Lacey Quintero

It seems my daughter has ended the Milestone. She's eating again (full appetite), she's taking her regular one short nap again, singing the ABC's and Twinkle, Twinkle, and overall a happier/cooperative/more independent toddler! We are 8 days past 23 months when adjusted for due date. – Lacey Quintero

Conflict Resolution

No change for this one, but big changes are in store!

Activities

Memory games

Go get an object from another room games, e.g., a favorite toy (child must remember this is their task the entire time as they get the object)

Singing songs (to eventually learn the whole song)

Transferring activities (with hands, spoons, a baster, tongs, or other utensils using water, rice, beans, or other objects) from one container to another

Sensory bins for further transferring practice

Stringing activities

Transfer water with a sponge; show how a sponge can be used to clean up spills

Put together open-ended building sets, such as wooden train tracks

Phonics Island

We introduced a tablet at this milestone. I found great value in electronic devices. They can keep up with a child longer than I can. You can put only what you are comfortable with on the device. Using it to teach letter sounds is one example of where an electronic device really shines. We used an app called *Phonics Island*. It simply asks the child to pop a balloon that sounds like [whatever letter sound]. I found a tablet could keep up with a child's desire to do this a lot longer than I could. The child needs to have done the concrete to abstract activities as described previously (in the milestone of Symbolic Thought) in order to understand what letters are before using the app. There is also a Memory Game in *Phonics Island*, where cards are turned face down and the child finds matching letters, that I found children can do surprisingly well at this young age. On *Phonics Island*, there is also a tracing letters activity the child can do. At this milestone, with such a big memory increase, the child can learn all 26 letters and their letter sounds. *Phonics Island* also helped to teach my children both upper-case and lower-case letters.

I would sing "The 'A's on the bus go 'ah ah ah' ... just like 'ant'" to reinforce that "A" is the name of the letter but "ah" is the sound of the letter, when they learned letter sounds.

Starfall Academy

Another app that I liked was *Starfall Academy*. While there is a yearly subscription for it, I found it was worth it, because it has a wide variety of activities. I once went to teach my son, a preschooler at the time, even/odd numbers, and he informed he already knew them and called up *Starfall Academy* to show me. There are many reading activities on *Starfall Academy* that my daughter enjoyed doing.

Memory Games

Maria Montessori describes in her books activities where some of the materials are put in a different room and the child has to go get them. For instance, have the child get a red color tablet. The child has to remember as they walk over that they are getting the red one. A similar activity at home can easily be recreated, using any toy at all.

Sensory Bins

A sensory bin is a bin, pan, or other container filled with a material such as rice, sand, dry beans, fake dirt, or another base material. Other objects such as cups, spoons, sea shells, toy trucks, figurines etc., can be added. Many parents like to make sensory bins with a theme, such as a holiday theme like Halloween or a theme of a place such as the beach. Let the child scoop and pour the material. A sandbox outside, with many tools to play with, is its own sensory bin and can be enjoyed by children who are younger than one year old. A sensory bin is a great open-ended toy that can build the child's attention span while also building fine motor skills.

Stringing Activities

Stringing activities can help develop a child's fine motor ability and hand-eye coordination. It is ideal at this milestone, now they are developing better fine motor control.

Here are some stringing activity ideas:

Thread shoe string through large tubular pasta.

Push pipe cleaners through the holes in a colander.

Stick uncooked spaghetti into a lump of Play-Doh, and string Cheerios (or beads) onto the spaghetti. This is surprisingly fun!

Cars, Trains, and Airplanes

Every toddler has different interests, but one interest might be cars, trains, and/or airplanes. I much preferred wooden train tracks to plastic. They go together easier and they are usually modular (fit with each other). Children can put the train tracks together on their own, and they can create a different configuration every time they play.

Some other ideas of what to do with cars, trains, or airplanes:

Put masking tape on the floor for them to push their cars on or in between the lines.

Have them put the cars in a line. I found this made many children burst with laughter.

With model airplanes, have a book with those same airplanes and have them match the model to the picture. You can also make your own activity by printing out photos of the airplanes to match.

Practical Life Exercises

A major advantage of using Montessori methods in the home is that it naturally lends to doing many practical life exercises. One issue however is that homes are designed for adults, not children, whereas a Montessori classroom is entirely designed around the size of a child. A stool can help; I found children catch up quickly enough and love to be a part of helping with real and important stuff, even if they aren't quite big enough yet. Asking them to help you do things you are already doing is one possibility, depending on your time and willingness.

This is a list of activity ideas that they may be able to do at this milestone, when they have developed better fine motor control:

Cut a banana or hardboiled egg with a knife. A butter knife can be used. Cut it in half for them first so that it lies flat.

Help take care of a plant.

Get involved in cooking, such as making scrambled eggs or make frozen fruit popsicles together.

Put caps on pens and markers.

Play dress up and practice putting on bracelets, hats, shoes, and so on. Find many pieces of jewelry made out of different, fun, and pretty materials.

Screwing lids on jars. If you serve food family style on a table, where the food is out for them to serve themselves, children can practice unscrewing the lids of jars (such as on cashews) on a daily basis.

Help with laundry. Toddlers can put soap in; turn the washer or dryer on; push clothes baskets around; find their own clothes in the basket; and help hang clothes.

Use a handheld vacuum.

Use a mop or Swiffer.

Use a soapy sponge to clean up stains on a hardwood or tile floor.

Use a paper towel to dust off furniture

Practice using a spray bottle filled with water—great fun!

Use a fork and spoon on their own.

Use a flashlight.

Use tools (toy or real) and let the child practice screwing nuts on bolts or hammering.

Buckle seatbelts.

Your Child's Second Birthday

Happy birthday to your little one! At your child's second birthday, they may be able to memorize whatever song you sing at their birthday party. I liked to have them practice blowing out candles before their party by putting candles in Play-Doh, lighting them, and letting the child blow them out.

Toddler Milestone 5 – Persistence and Insistence

Starts: 2 years, 1 week
Most Intense: 2 years, 1 month
Ends: 2 years, 1 month, 1 week
Irritable Period Summary

Bossy, demanding, and whiny, e.g., mom has to sit on a particular chair or has to change their diaper a very particular way

Wants things done exactly the same way as days earlier, which may not be possible and may result in a meltdown, e.g., assemble a train track like another person did (and you don't know how they did it)

Won't nap, stalls at naptime

Clumsy (may be from not napping)

Takes clothes off

Shows fear

Most Intense Period

The previously listed behaviors start out somewhat subtly and get much more intense at the most intense period

New Abilities Summary

Distinctive

Comes back to the same activity day after day and gets better at it each day

Very persistent at accomplishing a challenge, e.g., a jigsaw puzzle

Remembers how something was done from a few days ago

Variable

Very conversational

Counts up to 8 or 9

Speaks two sentences, e.g., "Hi, Mommy. It's nice to see you."

Can verbally state emotions

Notices emotions in others or in characters in a book involving the characters

Irritable Period Description

"Relentless" is a good way to describe the irritable period of this milestone. As with all toddler cognitive milestones, it seems to come way too soon. With every new one, I typically think, "Certainly not another one already?" But this one seems especially unrelenting, because of how very demanding, whiny, and let me just say it—outright annoying—that the child becomes. It gets especially intense slightly after 2 years, 1 month.

One thing to note is that some parents may not notice the irritable period until it is at its most intense. A working parent might not notice how demanding their child has become during diaper changes, because the child had most diaper changes while in the care of others throughout the day. A stay-at-home parent may notice the subtle signs of the irritable period sooner than this. If they are anything like me, they may be in denial that another one is happening again.

Bossy and whiny are good ways to describe this irritable period. With my son, I had to sit on a particular chair. When something didn't go the way my son thought it should, he would have a total meltdown. For instance, he would ask me to assemble train tracks the way his father would and, not knowing how that exactly was, I would disappoint him, and he would get angry. Or, as he was letting a hula hoop roll down our stairs, if it didn't roll the way he wanted, he would get very upset.

My daughter became whiny and demanding. Diaper changes were a nightmare. We had to do certain things the exact way she wanted, and we weren't allowed to put a diaper on her until she said so. I lost track of the number of times she pointed at me and said, "No!"

My daughter refused to nap for 2 weeks straight. She became very clumsy in the afternoons. She once fell off the side of a couch. It was hard to tell but it seemed like she fell because she had fallen asleep while standing up. This clumsiness may be a product of the cognitive growth, or the fact that she was not napping, which also may be from the cognitive growth.

New Abilities Description

With these new annoying behaviors also comes the positive behaviors to counter-balance them. Children are insistent and demanding at this milestone, but they are also persistent—giving further proof to the dual nature of cognitive growth spurts. My daughter took an interest in a 12-piece jigsaw puzzle. What especially impressed me was that she kept trying to do it day after day. After a few days of trial and error, she was able to complete this rather big challenge.

My daughter, after much counting practice, could accurately count up to 8 or 9—though other mothers report their children doing this at earlier ages. I noticed that she remembered the way we did something a few days earlier and wanted to do it the same exact way. My daughter became much more conversational, speaking effortlessly. She described many things as "beautiful" now. She became intensely interested in apps on her tablet. She did more academic activities on it, like tracing letters. My son started coloring in circles.

My daughter turned into a copycat and was able to verbalize emotions better. We had a children's book where a character noticeably looks sad. She was struck by it and kept pointing to it and asked what it was. I described the character's name and that it was a fire truck, but when I said "sad" she was finally satisfied with my answer.

Feedback

My step dad just passed away the month prior. Hailey was persistent and insisting that we visit him. She keeps asking where Papa is. She is continuously talking all day and night. – Christina

Toddler milestone 5 has started today. She is 2 years, 1.5 weeks. My daughter won't be entertained by anything. I usually put on a tv show while I make breakfast and that didn't even occupy her today. She has been whining all day. All of her usual activities (music, playdoh, stickers, coloring, reading, etc.) have only kept her attention for mere seconds before she is whining and climbing all over me again. Her usual limit-testing behaviors are in full force too. She's been ripping up our dog's foam bedding, climbing all over furniture, purposely making a mess with food/toys, and overall just not listening to anything I ask her to do. Can't wait until this over! – Lacey Quintero

We have clearly just ended toddler milestone 5. My Daughter is 25 months, 2 weeks, 2 days. – Lacey Quintero

Some new skills I noticed yesterday:

-I had my hands full with our new baby. I gave my daughter one of her drawings with pieces of scotch tape already attached to it. She was able to follow my directions from across the room to go tape it on the far wall. She struggled for a minute and for a few tries, but as I explained that she need to press down onto the part of the tape pieces that were touching the wall, she was able to finally do it.

-Yesterday on a car ride she started singing several whole songs and I could actually hear the words clearly. Previously, she would only sing Twinkle, Twinkle Little Star, which is her bedtime song. Now, she's singing the full alphabet song, Row, Row, Row Your Boat, and a few other classic nursery songs.

133

-She could previously count to about 14 by memory during the last [milestone] (but would always skip #5 for some reason). However, she could only count to 2 when actually counting objects. Now, she's correctly counting 6 objects.

-She knows her full name now, although she mispronounces our last name.

-A few days ago I took down some of her drawings from the fridge. I didn't think she'd notice the next morning, but sure enough, she saw the fridge and said her drawings were missing.

-Her memory has clearly improved. We talk about Easter happening in 3 days and she seems to better understand the concept of a calendar days count down until Easter. – Lacey Quintero

What a lifesaver to know I'm not alone or crazy! We are currently in [Milestone 5]. You nailed it with the bossy, whiny, and wanting things done the same way each day. Cecilia insists her dad or brothers push her around in her babies stroller, and they have to push it with both hands or she yells at them. Her vocabulary has exploded into being able to use several sentences back and forth to have an actual conversation. She shows fear at bedtime and through the night if she wakes up needing the bathroom. – Amber Kreeger

My son started acting weirdly fussy, he had just turned 25 months old. I checked out the [summary] and lo and behold he's right under the storm cloud. He has been so difficult. Used to lay down nicely for his diaper changes now he fights them, he even grabs the changing mat and tosses it away thinking we can't change him without it. He's been having a language explosion though, he knew lots of words before but only used them 1 or 2 times. Now he is repeating words he knows quite frequently and even stringing sentences together. – Alison, about her son Joel

Conflict Resolution

At this milestone children can no longer be as easily distracted or redirected. The parenting tools that worked at younger ages now start to lose their effectiveness. They now dig their feet in and won't let go of an idea they have. New conflict resolution tools are needed.

At first, I did not know how to respond to this. Surely, the answer could not be to always have things go the exact way my children wanted them to go—especially not having a ball roll exactly the way it did the time before. It's at this age that understanding how to validate emotions

134

becomes vital. Especially effective is knowing how to give in fantasy what you can't give in reality. If the child wants something that you just plain can't give, this is effective, as described by Dr. Ginott in *Between Parent and Child*. You might say, "I know you want the ball to roll a certain way. I wish it could roll that way many times in a row!"

It is still acceptable to just act—to put the kid in the car seat or pick them up to change their diaper. However, any parent can tell you it certainly is nicer to deal with a child who is not kicking and screaming. You can work towards calming a child down while doing these things that the child doesn't want to do. My primary tactic still was "distraction" as it was in previous milestones, but it was a more directed distraction. When they were younger I could make up anything whatsoever ("Hey, look at this caterpillar!") and get my children to cooperate as I, say, changed their diaper. Now, I had to make an educated guess as to what they wanted. When I figured out what it is they wanted though, it certainly helped. For us, it usually was talking about a favorite story. For instance, at bedtime, if they wanted another story, we would talk about the story while I got them ready for bed. This works at bedtime, getting in the car, out in public, etc.

I also noticed with both children that they showed more fear about things. My son told us he was scared of thunder. My daughter showed she was afraid to get on a tricycle. For both, this fear was new. Up until then, people we would meet for the first time would say about either of them that they seemed fearless. This is another reason to understand handling a child's emotions before this age, 2 years and 1 month.

I strongly recommend reading the book *Liberated Parents, Liberated Children* by Adele Faber and Elaine Mazlish or, alternatively, *Between Parent and Child* by Dr. Haim Ginott, who was their mentor. Both books are great. I liked *Liberated Parents, Liberated Children* because of its format. The authors hosted parenting classes and they describe the questions the parents had at each meeting. This book in particular thus addresses the questions and confusions a parent might have as they learn the approach originally put forth by Dr. Ginott. Dr. Ginott's classic is also of course fantastic. I try to read it once per year.

It is also most helpful to have your emotions under control. It is always powerful for me as a parent to ask myself, "What am I feeling right now?" before I respond to my children. It is the most efficient way to calm myself down within seconds. I learned how to have control over my emotions mainly from Dr. Tsabary's *The Awakened Family*. I found reading Dr. Tsabary's book gave me a calm, confident voice when speaking to my children, which they responded to really well. I believe her book is a must read.

   Sending you strength as you wade through this difficult, major milestone!

Activities

   Toys that they can try to master day after day

   Jigsaw puzzles, 12 pieces

   Tracing activities

   Counting loose objects

   Read books and talk about the emotions seen

Toddler Milestone 6 – Decision Making

Starts: 2 years, 1 month, 2 weeks
Most Intense: 2 years, 1 month, 3 weeks until 2 years, 2 months, 1 week
Ends: 2 years, 3 months
Irritable Period Summary

At first, just wants to be held, cuddled, or picked up a lot

Cries for seemingly no reason

Asks for help

Bossy, e.g., about where you are allowed to sit

Stubborn, e.g., might only wear one style of shirt

Fearful

Shows regret over past decisions, e.g., chose one pair of shoes then wants a different one while out

Plays jokes, e.g., hides things from you on purpose

Sleep disruptions

Clumsy

Most Intense Period

All of the above but at their worst

New Abilities Summary
Distinctive

Can make a choice after someone asks a question

Can alter their course if one way isn't working

Compares many things, e.g., big and small, or loud and quiet

Variable

Initiates conversations and activities a lot more

Initiate jokes and games with others

Irritable Period Description

At this irritable period, my daughter asked to be picked up a lot. She liked to get a hug and just rest on one of us for a bit. She sometimes cried, and we didn't know what was wrong. She said, "Help me, Help me," frequently.

She was insistent on sitting where she wanted and wanted to move other people sometimes. She just really threw her weight around. My children became fearful of things. Both children explicitly stated, noticeably, that they were scared of certain things and also hesitated to do some things.

My daughter became very stubborn. She always wanted to wear a particular style of shirt. She picked one pair of shoes to go out once, which were different than the normal pair that she usually wore, and then had a meltdown while out that she didn't have her normal pair of shoes on. I believe she was playing around with making decisions and then was suffering with regret.

There were sleep disruptions. My daughter became very clumsy. She could go from having a meltdown to being totally happy if we could guess what it was she wanted.

About one week shy of 2 years, 2 months, these behavioral features became intense, and this intensity lasted for about 2 weeks—until 2 years, 2 months, 1 week.

New Abilities Description

I named this milestone, which started around 2 years, 2 months, "Decision Making." My daughter could understand making a decision like, "You can walk or I will carry you. It's up to you."

She also showed she had the flexibility to try an alternative solution if one wasn't working out, such as flipping a different way in a book to find a picture. She could tell that she and I weren't communicating sometimes and would change what she said to accommodate it. I once had thought she was saying "Paint." She started to say, "White plate." This helped clarify it for me. Another time, she wanted more cake, and I told her she already had some. She started saying "Green, green." She specifically wanted some green frosting. I was able to give it to her.

She loved to initiate jokes and games. She would hide things and ask me to find them. She was a total ham. If you sang with her, she would tell you to stop. She would then clear an area for herself, then start singing like she was performing. When I walked into a room once, she said, "Auugh!," then fell over laughing, saying, "I scared Mommy!" It is possible that these were clues to her unique personality. I encourage you to look for clues to your child's unique personality in such unexpected moments.

It was very common for her to say, "What are you doing, Mommy?" or "What are you doing, John?" She also said, "Pretty loud!" when something was loud. She loved to compare things as big or small. She called her dad "Big Daddy." She called herself "Little Emily."

She could point to letters, give their letter sounds, and identify something that starts with the letters. She would say, "W. Wuh wuh wuh. Woody!"

Feedback

We just had baby #2. Hailey loves being a big sister. She is helpful with the baby and she wants to play with the baby. The baby was crying, and Hailey was playing with her toy ice creams and she decided that the baby needed one of her toy ice creams to stop crying and handed her an ice cream cone. – Christina

My daughter is totally in [milestone 6] and I'm going crazy. Doesn't want to go to bed, tantrums when she doesn't get her way, she wants to be carried instead of walking (like to/from the car or up/down the stairs), etc. We try to follow a peaceful parenting route but man, she gets me at my wits end sometimes. – Katie Brenner Broyles

Yes, your description of the 23/24 mo [milestone] and the 26 mo [milestone] is consistent with what we experienced. – Angela Laird

Confirming Toddler Milestone 6. Starting 2 yrs 1 month 2 weeks (adjusted for due date). Started off with nap disruptions for a few days. Then started waking one hour early for a few days. Then night waking began (haven't dealt with this since she was 13 months old), wakes up screaming and crying, she sounds scared when I ask her what's wrong. She asks for water, songs, and a bedtime stories for help. To fall back asleep. She doesn't fall back asleep immediately after doing another shortened bedtime routine to help her back asleep. She is still awake and asking to play with bubbles (blowing bubbles outside) when I keep telling her that bubbles is tomorrow after she wakes up. When she hurts herself she runs away screaming "no" instead of running to us for soothing like she normally does. – Lacey Quintero

Conflict Resolution

At this milestone, giving a choice where inaction is not an option becomes a new conflict resolution technique. This is different than giving limited choices, because one of the choices has to be what you will do if the child does *not* make a choice. An example may be, "You can get in the car seat or I will put you in." I learned this from the book *How to Talk so Kids Will Listen* by Adele Faber and Elaine Mazlish. It may sound like a threat, but it's not. The choice tells the child "You need to do something" in an obvious way and promises a contingent follow-up of gentle action, not insults or punishment. It's better than threatening to take away Santa Claus. It is also better than nagging. It is kind and firm. My experience was most times, the child will say, "Ok! I will [do as asked]! I don't want to be picked up!"

When my daughter had the meltdown in public that she didn't have a different pair of shoes on (even though she previously wanted the ones she did have on), we talked about the other pair of shoes and how great and awesome they were. This is the tactic of giving children in fantasy what they can't have in reality. This calmed her down a lot.

Activities

Anything where they can make a decision

Asking questions so they can show off their knowledge

Sorting objects by length, width, etc.

Matching the first letter of a word to its object

Let Them Show Off Their Knowledge

My daughter loved to answer any kind of question, such as "What color is Thomas the Train?" as if to show off her knowledge. She would delight in spending time thinking about the right answer and would compete with her brother, insisting that he not answer a question so that she could. This is fun for children, as they happily spend time deciding what the right answer is.

Sort Objects by Length, Width, or Size

Classic Montessori activities such as the pink cubes, rods, or brown stairs are great. I only bought the pink cubes and used them as stairs, instead of buying the brown stairs. I used the pink cubes as stairs at first, as it is easier to build stairs than a tower. I facilitated my children by letting them drive small toy cars down the stairs. This serves as a control of error (something built in to the material itself to let the child see if they have done an activity correctly or not) to show if the stairs kept going downward as they pushed the cars down. If a big cube was out of place, they would not be able to continue to push the toy car down.

Sorting Activities

Here are some sorting activity ideas:

Simply giving children an egg carton or muffin tin and something to sort (marbles, coins, buttons, beans, pasta, plastic eggs, etc.) without suggestion of what to do (Let them amaze you with how they sort!)

Sorting objects that are similar shapes

Organizing shoes in the shoe area (also a practical life skill)

Playing a game of picking out marbles of a certain color; filling up a toy dump truck with them; driving the truck on masked tape to a paper plate; dumping the marbles. Sorting, filling, moving, and pouring!

Match the First Letter of an Object to the Object

Matching a movable letter to an object whose name starts with that letter is something that you can do at this young age now that they can make a decision. I found my daughter did not do this for another month, but, given that children can make a decision starting at this milestone, I believe this is the earliest they may be able to do this.

The first thing you will need are movable letters. I cannot stress enough the importance of having an organizer for the letters. It lays out the letters nicely for the child to get and brings a lot of clarity to the activity. I did not have an organizer when I did this activity with my first child, but I had obtained one by the time my second child was this age, and it made a big difference. Plastic letter tile organizers exist and are much less expensive than wood. It is ideal that the letters are the same color. I wish manufacturers would stop making letters and other things multi-colored. We bought a set of magnetic letters and then spray painted them such that the consonants were purple and the vowels were yellow. Most letter tile organizers come with letters. I would recommend buying them as a package.

Identifying the first letter of a word is the easiest step for a child to start building words. The easiest activity to do with a child is to find the most simple, clear, vivid book you can find that has a letter and a word that starts with that letter next to it. Nothing compares to Dick Bruna's *b is for bear*. This book is no longer in print but used copies are available from online sellers. On the first page of this book, there is an "a" and opposite of this is a bright, clear apple—and that's all there is. Point to the "a" and say "aah" and point to the apple and say "apple." "aa, apple." "bb, bear." "cc, castle." There are two things you say per page, and that is it.

The next activity is to grab a movable letter and match it to its letter using the same book you used for the previous activity. This is so easy. Right? It gets the child used to selecting a letter from the organizer and then putting it back. Doing all 26, which is quite a lot, in alphabetical order makes it easy for the child to know where the letters go. In doing this easy matching activity, they are noticing thoroughly how "bbbb" is the first part of "bear." Getting to this point is huge. The child can see the connection between the letter and the sound in the word. I like to use a book for this especially (as opposed to a hand-made activity), because it, like previous reading activities described, draws the child into books. Hearing a letter sound while saying a word with the sound might help your child identify them better. Trying to make an isolated "b" sound is hard. It's always "buh," not "bbbb." This activity is simultaneously stage three of retrieving a letter sound, and stage one of introducing the idea that words are made up letter sounds.

For stage two, the child is put to a harder test. Here is the easiest activity you can do. Get three letters and objects which match those letters with the first letter of their name. The child then matches the three letters to the objects. This should be very easy at this point, but a nice, healthy challenge for them. Give a demonstration of this at first and don't ask the child to do the lesson until the day after the demonstration. My daughter could do this handily at 2 years, 3 1/2 months.

If working with a word whose first letter sound is not represented by the typical letter sound, go with what the first letter of the word sounds like. For instance, giraffe would match with "j."

Matching games using books are also ideal where you match for instance "s" to Cinderella's picture.

You do your child a great favor by staying with these activities for weeks. I find children have trouble finding the second letter of most words, such as the "a" in "cat." I propose this may be because vowels are harder to differentiate than consonants. "K" and "M" sound a lot different from each other than do "E" and "I." So, work on every single letter possible until you are confident they can hear a letter sound and retrieve the letter. Do consonants first, and then work on vowels.

Toddler Milestone 7 – Deliberate Rearranging and Creation

Starts: 2 Years, 3 Months, 3 Weeks
Most Intense: Around 2 years, 4 months and again at 2 years, 5 months
Ends: 2 years, 5 months, 2 weeks
Irritable Period Summary

Fear of abandonment

Confusion of fake things as real things

Doesn't nap

Bossy, e.g., about diaper changes or where you are allowed to stand

Defiant

Possessive of primary caregiver

Major meltdowns

About one meltdown per day in between the two peaks

Most Intense Period

There are two peaks at this one. It may be two overlapping milestones but no real relief was seen in between them. A strong fear of abandonment and confusion of fake and real things around 2 years, 4 months and another intense period at 2 years, 5 months with less intense behavior in between

New Abilities Summary

Distinctive

Follows a pattern to build something, e.g., tangrams

Pretends to be a favorite character, e.g., Snow White or Thomas the Train

Puts on a play based on a book

Moves around furniture and items in the house

Builds train tracks or other sets on their own

Plays with language; very fluent

You can see children thinking

Irritable Period Description

Just shy of 2 years, 4 months, my daughter clearly entered an irritable period. At first, she showed it when she did not want me to leave her with our babysitter. Then she refused diaper changes in the morning. It was a nightmare, really. This one is intense and long.

My daughter was very bossy. For instance, she would insist that I stand in the upstairs toy room and wait while she walked downstairs.

This irritable period was at its first worst time around 2 years, 4 months. My daughter got really mad that I threw away something in the garbage, which is a fear of abandonment.

I saw also a deep confusion between what is fake and real, such as how my daughter once had a total meltdown over what she thought were real golf balls on a video game. A story that I told on my Facebook page, The Observant Mom:

Holy moly is it a rough morning here. My daughter 2, has clearly been going through something. It started about 2 weeks ago and it's been increasingly more difficult. I hope it's at its worst now. She is twenty-eight months almost on the dot.

Today, my son, 4, got out the Wii Fit and played a golf game on it. The character on the screen drives the golf ball towards a putting green. My daughter all of a sudden had a total meltdown. She kept asking where the balls were going and kept trying to push the stand the TV was on over. She thought the balls were going "behind the TV" and just had a total meltdown over it.

I was reminded about a story I read about a lady who dealt with an aging parent who had dementia. When the elderly person would start to worry that he lost his wallet, the caregiver would try showing him his wallet to prove it was not gone. It didn't work. She eventually learned to just indulge the thought and not try to prove him wrong.

My son, 4, tried doing exactly this. "There are no balls behind the tv!" Then he showed her, "Look! They are on the tv!" This made it so much worse.

I tried indulging her a bit, or, I should say, acknowledging the worry. "You are worried about the balls?" "You think they are behind the tv?" It didn't work. She kept relentlessly trying to push the stand.

Conveniently, all of her lovies, which are almost always in her bed, were missing this morning. Did I mention the crying baby (4 months old, also in an irritable period) also? What eventually calmed her down is when I put on nursery rhyme songs for her.

Though my son focused more on proving to my daughter her concern was of no worry, I was thrilled when he said, "This first day of Valentine's Day is really rough!" (We were doing a Valentine's Day activity that started that day.) I was so pleased that he recognized that it's not that his sister is permanently difficult, but that this was all very temporary. I am thrilled he picked up on this and put it in such perspective. What a way to keep your cool.

It's my hope to spread this thought to many others: everything is always so temporary.

My daughter took a nap maybe once or twice per week during this irritable period. She had many meltdowns. The majority of most days were actually decent, but there were certain flare-ups at certain times. She definitely did not like not getting her own way.

It was difficult like this from 2 years, 4 months all the way to after 2 years, 5 months. I did notice that after 2 years, 4 months, there was a slight let up in the most intense period, but it never fully dissipated, and it was intense again around 2 years, 5 months. The period in between was not as bad as these two points, with maybe one meltdown per day— but it was reliably one per day. It may be two overlapping cognitive growth spurts right on top of each other, I really am not sure, and I wasn't able to differentiate new skills between these time periods. For the purpose of this body of work, I am counting them as one. It lasted until 2 years, 5 months, and 2 weeks.

New Abilities Description

At this milestone, my daughter was constantly rearranging things. She would flip the lights on and off. She moved chairs around. She wrapped herself in curtains and hid under rugs. She climbed on top of me and tried to open my eyes if they were closed. She was not only talking fluently but making up mishmashes of songs, mixing one with the other.

From what I observe, children have a drive to rearrange their environment, and in bigger ways than before. It's is as if they have an idea in their head of what it should be and they need to make it a reality. In this way, this may be the beginning of creative imagination. It is interesting that in the irritable period, they greatly confuse fantasy and reality, and in the new ability period, they have a drive to recreate what seems to be a vision in their mind. The cognitive growth spurts, I find, are often dual natured.

Both of my children really started creating at this milestone. I had bought wood blocks for my son at an early age. They laid dormant up until this milestone. This is what I wrote when my son was 2 years, 4 months, 2 weeks from the due date on a personal Facebook photo:

147

For years, these wooden blocks sat easily available to John but unused. Then, as of a few days ago, it's all he wants to do and he makes elaborate structures with them. This is how all of his development has gone: It lies dormant ... dormant ... dormant ... dormant ... then BOOM, it explodes.

I call a certain type of activity an "abstract to concrete" activity. It is using something that is usually drawn on paper and building something from it. Examples are acting out a play based on a script, building something based on a blueprint, or playing music based on a sheet of music. I found this skill begins at this age. My daughter's favorite activity was to act out stories from books, using either figurines or herself as the actress. Her first one was Snow White. She seemed to think she *was* Snow White. She would ask us to kiss her to wake her up from naps. My son put a magnet on the front of his train once and said it was a "snowplow", which is from a Thomas the Train story. Fantasy and reality are a blur. This is why I would never recommend seeing something scary, like a fake shark, with the child. Keep fake food that they might try to eat, such as if it is made out of Styrofoam, out of their reach.

My daughter could put together a puzzle that requires knowing what the picture looks like alone. It was a puzzle of blocks that don't interlock. Each piece is a cube and on each side of the cube is a different picture to make a different puzzle, for six in all. To do this puzzle, she had to have a picture in her head, an abstract idea, and was able to recreate it, in the concrete form of the puzzle. She also took an interest in tangrams, where objects are built out of shapes. Using just triangles and squares, based on a drawn pattern, she would build a "candle." She worked off of a pattern (abstract to concrete).

An obvious skill, which lends itself to think children have much more conscious control over what they do, is how you can tell the child is thinking about something. There are thoughts and ideas that you can see the child mull over. My daughter once played a "follow what I do game" with my husband. She would stick her tongue out, then he would; or clap, and then he would. I could clearly see in between activities that she was thinking about what to do next, as she darted her eyes around while thinking.

Both of my older children loved the part in *Green Eggs and Ham* by Dr. Seuss where the "mean" guy is thinking about eating green eggs and ham, finally. I said, "He's thinking about it!" on this page, and they were both struck by it.

My daughter did many Montessori activities with complete ease. She rearranged the pink cubes into both a stair and a tower. She arranged rods of increasing length into order. I had her match those rods to drawn representations of the rods, and she did it handily. She once found a random hollow box made of wood meant to hold a logic puzzle and found the exact Montessori pink cube to fit in it. She could easily get the right cube on demand.

Feedback

Hailey has decided to rearrange all her toys. She had a toy kitchen in the living room and she started to move it to her room. She says she "needs more space" in the living room for her other toys. She seems to have a greater understanding of things as well. – Christina

Literally to the day 2 years, 3 months, and 3 weeks we hit [milestone 7] like a freight train. Her sleep has gone to absolute rubbish. Waking often and not resettling without me nearby. She is way more demanding and clingy than before, oh and the whining!!!! – Jodie Abraham Asim

My son turned 2 years 4 months yesterday... Omg. I love my son, but honestly don't really like him right now. – Erica Carpenter Gutierrez

The fear of abandonment coupled with major meltdowns AND the ridiculous heat in the UK at the moment. I. Am. Going. Crazy. We've gone past the worst now I think (2 years 5 months 3 weeks) and the last 2 weeks his language has been growing more fluent daily. – Anjuli Leahy

Conflict Resolution

It remains OK to pick children up and do what you must. If they refuse a diaper change, you can simply pick them up and do it. I often try to talk to the child about something the child likes, such as a favorite story. Being calm and aware of your own emotions is key. Sending you strength and patience for this one!

This is a good milestone, where they start to build so much, to start giving children descriptive praise. My chapter "Dealing with the Child's Emotions" has more details on how to give descriptive praise. When they create something, simply notice things about it. If they build a simple structure from Mega Bloks, say, "I noticed you put a blue one on top and a red one on the bottom." At this age, they are playing with making deliberate creations. If you notice that they made a deliberate choice, it will be deeply satisfying to them. At a slightly older age than this, I did this for my daughter by telling her I noticed she colored something in purple. She carried around her "picture" for days after that.

Activities

Let the child "boss" you around in a fun way.

Read *Green Eggs, and Ham*, pausing at the point where the mean guy thinks about eating the green eggs and ham and say, "He's thinking about it!"

Let them build!

Anything where the child can build something is great. I found this was the beginning of my son's passion for building train tracks and my daughter's passion for putting on plays. These served as a great calming "go to happy place" for them when they went through future cognitive growth spurts. If you can find something that your child loves, I recommend feeding this passion. I hear successful artists sometimes say, "I have been writing and telling stories since I was two!" Take notice of what interests them. The activities below are just some ideas.

Putting on a Play

Putting on a play, using a book or movie that the child is already familiar with, helps develop the skill of recreating a story, develops reading comprehension, and goes a long way towards emotional regulation and eventual conflict resolution skills. Using a book with pictures in it is nice because you can open it up and follow along with it. You can use any story you like using any form you like. We sometimes used dolls or figurines as actors or ourselves.

Building Something from a Picture

We had a "Sort and Match" toy sold by Guidecraft. It comes with a board with pegs on it that the child can hang parts on to make something, such as a truck. It comes with a few suggested patterns. The child can do this particular toy at a younger age, but they likely put on the pieces randomly. Now they might build the trucks that match the pattern. You can help them by placing the pieces on the patterns before building them on the board. Don't feel limited to this toy. I offer it as an example. If they aren't interested in building the exact patterns, please save it for another day and let them play with it as they want.

Materials to Build with

There are so many building materials to give a child. I had to actively stop myself from buying so many. Here are some ideas: Wood blocks, LEGO's, Mega Bloks, Quercetti Tubation toy (or any Quercetti product), and Crazy Forts.

Flower Arranging

Using real or fake flowers and different-sized vases, the child can make flower arrangements.

Musical Instruments

Children may enjoy creating their own music. If you get a musical instrument, I would recommend getting some that make music, and not ones that just pretend to make music. Some instruments are more sophisticated than others. Why not invest in one that is sturdy yet can be played somewhat accurately? I recommend this thinking about their future advancement. Alternatively, rolling up a piece of paper into a cone shape to make a "trumpet" works. If you think this might drive you crazy, maybe save this idea for a different time or place. I found most musical instruments surprisingly tolerable.

Moldable Compound

Play-Doh or modeling compound of any sort is perfect for a child who want to deliberately create things. Salt dough can be used, which can then be baked in the oven for semi-permanent creations. Kinetic Sand might work well for you. We had an issue with Play-Doh getting everywhere and being found by my infant. Kinetic Sand can still hold shape somewhat and when it fell, simply ground into the carpet, such that an infant can't get it, and could be cleaned up with a vacuum (though it may cause discoloration). Getting an indoor/outdoor rug, which is made of plastic and can be cleaned easily but still looks pretty good, for your play area might help this.

Molding some type of modeling compound has everything: fine motor skills, using a pattern to cut out shapes, learning about shapes, using tools such as scissors and pizza cutters, learning colors, and, of course, making art.

Activities to do:

Make snakes and balls out of the dough

Get tools that cut the dough in various ways, including child-safe scissors

Make shapes with small cookie cutters

Make simple 3-D objects such as bananas or eggs

Have examples of what to make that you and your child can follow

Let them make new clothes for figurines they have

Yoga or Other Movement Activities

Yoga might be one activity your children may enjoy, in which they put their bodies into a deliberate position based on a picture in a book or the example of another person. Many books designed for toddlers show yoga moves.

Here are other deliberate movement ideas:

Walk the line by putting tape down on the floor. Treat it like a balance beam. Add complication such as carrying something in their hands or heads while they do it or add music.

Ride a bike on a line. A balance bike is a great way to introduce children to a bike. I strongly preferred the one made by Strider.

Hop. If a floor is tiled, hop from square to square.

Jump over a rope.

Make a balance beam out of a wooden 2x4.

A set of rings for developing upper arm strength. These are available at gymnastic centers, which often offer preschool playdates.

Basic exercises like arm circles.

Outdoor obstacles courses.

Toddler Milestone 8 – Sequence of Events

Starts: 2 Years, 6 Months, 1 Week
Most Intense: 2 years, 7 Months
Ends: 2 years, 7 months, 2 weeks
Irritable Period Summary

Starts out sweet and subtle at first: wants lovey or to cuddle

A desire to stay up until very late at night, talking

Deliberately tells mistruths, e.g., Mommy is daddy, hides things and says lost them

Refuses naps, even though very sleepy

Very jealous

Bossy, e.g., about where you are allowed to sit

Will not want to leave a fun activity, such as being at the playground

Most Intense Period

Jealous and bossy about their primary caregiver, may hit or throw to separate primary caregiver from others, may not let primary caregiver move. A really big meltdown can be expected at or slightly after 2 years, 7 months, especially if you try to leave a place

New Abilities Summary
Distinctive

Understands sequences of events: "First this, then this"

Understands "yesterday," "today," and "tomorrow"

Remembers past events and wants to talk about them again

Uses the word "because," e.g., "I am not going to cry, because I am happy"

Variable

Beginning steps to sounding out letter sounds to read a word

Beginning concern to solve problems/help others but without particulars, e.g., a baby is crying and they say, "We need to help the baby!"

Beginning awareness of right and wrong but first shows up as playful games where they intentionally say the wrong answer

Irritable Period Description

For us, this irritable period started at 2 years, 6 months, 1 week. It was very sweet and subtle at first. My toddler simply wanted me to be near her and to cuddle. She took her lovies everywhere. It escalated, however, into an intense period right at 2 years, 7 months. She got very jealous. If I sat with her baby brother, she would bring me a book and sometimes even throw it at me. She was insistent about telling me where I was allowed to sit. It was outright frustrating and annoying to deal with. Sending you a pallet full of patience for this one.

My daughter also liked to play around with the idea of truth or not truth. As an example, I would say "Here's your doggie," and she would say, *"That's not doggie!"* She did this all the time. I asked her once who I was holding. I asked, "Is it Emily?" She said, *"That's not Emily!"* I then started rattling off different names: Cinderella, Snow White, Dory, Belle, etc. When I would occasionally say "Emily?" she would pause and dart her eyes around, clearly recognizing that it was the right answer—and then of course say, *"No!"*

I'd like to make a note about children who lie during the irritable period of a cognitive growth spurt. Everything in their perceptual awareness is changing and they are likely in disbelief of it. Imagine you saw what you thought to be Bigfoot walking through your house. Everything you've been taught has led you to understand that Bigfoot is a legend. And, yet, you saw it! You might say, "I, no ... that's not Bigfoot!" You would *verbalize* your confusion. I imagine this is how children are when they see something completely new and opposite of what their previous understanding of the world knew to be true.

My daughter did not want to leave fun activities. We had major issues with getting her to get out of the bathtub or when we were leaving the playground.

New Abilities Description

At the very start of this milestone, I sat down outside with a drink. My daughter begged me to come play in the sandbox with her. I told her, "I am going to drink my drink then come join you." She watched me take one sip and said, "You drank it! Now come on!" This alerted me to the fact that she could understand "First this, then that" about a "routine" that was new, i.e., not a routine done repeatedly.

My daughter developed an understanding of "yesterday" and "tomorrow."

My daughter would drink her drink and at the end say, "I'm finished!", recognizing the end of an event. She could remember an event that happened previously and talk about it.

An especially exciting development is best explained by when my daughter, after I said she might cry, said, "I'm not going to cry, because … I'm *happy!*" It was the first time she said the word "because." Since then, she used it often. "Because" implies cause and effect—"This, because of this." This is also a sequence of events. I am not going to cry, an action, because I am happy, my internal state. As is typical of milestones after the milestone of Decision Making, it is a very conscious and deliberate statement.

My daughter started to sound out words such as "jjj eee ttt, jet!" It is hard to tell if this is a product of this milestone or the last one, but being able to put things in sequence seems relevant to this new ability.

She said once after our infant was crying, "We need to help Henry!" This might be the very first sign of empathy. In the next milestone, the child can verbalize a more exact solution, e.g., the baby might need a bottle.

Feedback

We used a home hospice to put our pug to sleep after he could not walk and was not eating. We told Hailey that our dog was going to go to a farm. Later that night Hailey asked Daddy, "Daddy, you're sad? Because Bubba went to the farm? The doctor came to take him in a box?" We explained to her that he did have to go to the farm, but the doctor took him in a basket and not a box. She said, "It's OK Daddy" and gave him a hug. – Christina

Hi, we are just starting [milestone 8], so far I can see challenges with falling asleep at nap time and night time, understanding and using today and tomorrow. She remembers things that happened a while back and started making up stories about characters. – Alexandra LaFontaine

Well hello [milestone 8]. This describes what's going on perfectly. He is so clingy and whiny lately. Oh, and fighting bed time with a vengeance, thinking of every excuse he can to stall a little longer. – Shelly Lewis

Conflict Resolution

Now that children can remember past, present, and future, or are working on it, they will know that if you leave a fun place, they are leaving and won't go back. During or soon after this milestone, you may witness a meltdown if you try to leave, say, the playground. In fact, I

155

would be so bold as to say you can expect a really big meltdown at around exactly 2 years, 7 months. It's all a new awareness to them, so, empathy and creative methods to handle it are in order. My daughter once refused to get out of the bathtub and had a huge meltdown. When I gave her in fantasy what she could not have in reality, by wishing her room was one big bathtub, I was able to calm her down. This is the story I told on my Facebook page, The Observant Mom:

My 2 ½ year old had a really big meltdown today. It was time for a nap, but she insisted on taking a bath. I was like, well, it sometimes is really hard to get her in the bath, so why not do it now. So we took a bath. Then I finally asked her to get out. She got out willingly, but then wanted back in the bath when she realized I was trying to dress her. I tried bringing out some of her favorite things, such as videos of *Frozen*, but it wasn't working. I tried a weak, "I understand. I wish we could go into the bath too." I had the thought to just let her cry, but I tried that a few days ago and I knew it could go on for a really long time. No, this one needed some big tools.

I tried leaning into her wish as hard as I could. I said to her I wished her bedroom were one big bathtub and she were swimming in it. I wished there were bubbles as big as her laundry basket. I wished Dory were there; and Nemo; and Marlin; and Mr. Ray. She started to calm down. I let her sit with me for a bit. I asked if I could put a diaper on. She said yes!

I put her to bed and she took a long, hard nap.

I remember doing this exactly with my son at around this age. We were out and he wanted a drink in a white cup and all we had was a yellow cup. I wished we had a white cup as big as the moon and we could launch a rocket to space and get the drink out of the moon size *white* cup. He finally started laughing so hard and took the drink out of the yellow cup.

I wish I could find how old my son was, but he definitely was right around the same age as my daughter. I absolutely think this was a cognitive growth spurt. My daughter was 2 years, 7 months on the dot almost. I would go so far as to say that anyone with a 2 year, 7-month-old will experience at least one big meltdown like this.

Note: I had the good fortune of finally finding a document which was dated and, thus, I could find out how old my son was when the above happened. He was 2 years, 7 months, 3 weeks. It was this exact milestone.

Now that children understand a past event and hold it in their mind, they may ask you to repeat the event over and over. I found my toddler especially wanted to retell stories where she was in pain or fear for some reason. For instance, I ran into a store with her in the rain once and she lost her shoe. I retrieved it, but she was in exasperated tears while I went to get it. Afterwards, she asked to tell this story over and over. This is a healthy thing to do. Dr. Siegel in *The Whole-Brain Child: 12 Revolutionary Strategies to Nurture Your Child's Developing Mind* describes retelling an event over and over again after something traumatic happens, slowly at first, to take the sting out of the past memory. "Storytelling" is a new tool that can be used.

Activities

Put a calendar near their bed and cross off each day at night to help enforce the idea of today, yesterday, and tomorrow. Drawing a picture of what happened each day can also help.

Books with pictures and mostly phonetic words next to them. They may start to recognize that the particular order of the letters makes a word at this milestone. Use movable letters to match the words.

Putting Letters in Sequence to Make a Word

Now that the child can put things in order better, putting letters together to make a word is an ideal activity. As always, give an easy assist to help the child. I had a book with a word and its picture with it. I then had my child spell out the word, using movable letters, while having the word right in front of him to help. This is the first stage of stringing a word together. In the picture below, the letters are traced and movable letters are matched to the letters.

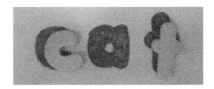

A great way to go to stage two is to use Microsoft Word or any other word processor and let children make up their own words. At first, they probably make up nonsense words—remember, misbehavior is growth! I find in time they start spelling actual words. I was greatly surprised when my daughter did this activity completely by herself that I found this:

AVADOGPIGFROGDDDDDDDDPPPPPUUUUUUYY
YYYYYYBBBBBBBBBBBLLLLHHHHHHHSSSSSLLLLL
LLLLLLLLLLLLLLLLLLLLLLLLLLLLLLLLMMMMMNNN
NNNNNCCCCCCCCCCCCCCCCCCCCCCCCCCCCCCCCC
CCCCCCCCCCCCCCCCCCCCCCCCCCCCCCCCCCCCCC
CCCCCCCCCCCCCCCCCCCCCCCCCCCCCCCCCCCCCC
CCCCCCCCCCCCCCCCCCCCCCCCC

Peppa Pig

Peppa Pig is a book series by Scholastic. I will not be the first to notice that children just shy of three years old love it, but let me point out how well it is in alignment with children's development at this age. There is a book in the series called *The Story of Peppa Pig*. Peppa's little brother George loses his dinosaur out in the mud when they rushed in suddenly after hearing thunder. George is distraught and Peppa helps him. This aligns with this milestone, where a child remembers past events, and a typical issue a child of this age might face. This book can easily grow with a child in the next milestones, such as how Peppa shows empathy towards her brother George, rightly acts to try to find his missing dinosaur (Budding Morality), and *loves* to immerse herself in muddy puddles.

Toddler Milestone 9 – Creative Problem-Solving

Starts: 2 Years, 7 Months, 3 Weeks
Most Intense: 2 years, 8 months
Ends: 2 years, 8 months, 2 weeks
Irritable Period Summary

Refuses naps, screams about being left alone

Keeps stalling at bedtime to do "just one more" thing

Very particular, e.g., insists on wearing a particular shirt, dress, or pants

Refuses to move to solve a very simple problem, e.g., a toy is a few feet away but the child won't get it but instead will cry for it, as if paralyzed to do it

Shows regret over the solution they originally picked, e.g., agrees that one solution is OK, such as dad can turn the light off, but they have a change of mind (and gets upset) a few seconds or minutes later when they seem to realize what is going on, because they wanted to do it

Seemingly paralyzed to answer a question, e.g., what movie would you like

Jealous if their caregiver gives attention to another child or person

Tries to separate primary caregiver from anyone or anything else that has the child's attention or who is not the child

Doesn't let you leave their side

Asks to cuddle (some of the behaviors are cute!)

Most Intense Period

Jealous, demanding, won't let you freely move, in seeming disbelief of what is going on, paralyzed to act

New Abilities Summary
Distinctive

Can come up with solutions to new problems that arise, e.g., if they notice it is cloudy, they might get an umbrella

Attempts to solve much more complex problems without help, e.g., putting batteries in a remote control

Can correct themselves on the spot better, e.g., they say something
wrong and you say it the right way, they say it then the right
way

Can match a song to what is going on, e.g., sing "Rain, rain, go
away" when it is raining

Color objects properly

Make up a play about someone helping someone else

Identify themselves as "thinking"

Say, "I don't know"

Growing but still developing empathy, or, rather, concern for others

Irritable Period Description

A most irritating behavior during this milestone is a refusal to take
simple steps to solve a problem. With both of my children, they would
want something, but seem to be completely paralyzed to get it. For
instance, a toy might be but two feet away, and they would cry and
scream for it, but they wouldn't simply go pick it up. My son seemed
unable to answer the question, "Which movie would you like to watch?"
Other mothers report how their children show regret over a previously
agreed to solution to solve a problem, such as how their child would
agree to let a parent turn off a light, but when the parent did, the child
had a meltdown, because they wanted to do it.

My daughter was very jealous if anyone had my attention. She
would try to separate me from the person, saying, "No! My Mommy!"
She never wanted me to leave her. She stalled at bedtime and refused
naps. She became very particular about what clothes to wear. There
were only two pairs of pants that she would agree to wear. She was
highly, highly, highly demanding. Some days it felt like the requests or
demands for my attention were constant. She once demanded we go to
the grocery store. There was no not going to the grocery store.

My son started to frequently ask us to come snuggle with him after
putting him to bed. One time, he grabbed the transmitter for his baby
monitor, yelled into it, "Mommy! I want to snuggle! Goodbye," and set
it down. Really: the irritable periods can be cute!

New Abilities Description

With the irritating behavior comes the amazing behavior. As often
was the case, it was dual natured. Though children won't take simple
steps to solve a problem in the irritable period, in the new abilities
period, they make steps in attempting to solve very complex problems.

160

For instance, my daughter figured out, almost on her own and on the spot, how to put batteries into a remote control. The most unique skill to this milestone is the ability to see a new problem arise and come up with a solution. For instance, my daughter once looked outside, and said, "It's cloudy! We need an umbrella!"

Both of my older children would start matching songs to events going on. If it was raining, they might start singing, "Rain rain, go away, come again another day." It was soon after this age that my daughter got good at selecting the proper color for an object, e.g., color Ariel's hair red (*The Little Mermaid*).

In the last milestone, children can remember a sequence of events, even ones that were new to them. For instance, "I am going to finish my drink, then we can do [what they wanted.]" This sequence of events may be critical to this problem-solving milestone. In the last milestone they can think, "I am using an umbrella because it is raining." Now they can say, "It is raining so I need to get an umbrella."

While my son was busy solving problems on his own, my daughter loved to ask for help. She would play the damsel in distress over and over. I have to think this is one way of solving a problem: "If I have a problem, and ask for help, will people come help me?" She found that her brother would routinely come help her and so would people at the playground. For me, personally, I had an issue with this at first, because I believe in independence. But I recognize what a value it is to have trust that, if you need help, other people may come to help you. This is certainly a benevolent view of people. So, I indulged her calls for help. I would say, "Look at how abundant the world is with people willing to help you!" In her defense, she did often solve problems on her own at times.

A classic symptom of cognitive growth spurts is disrupted sleep at night. Many times my son wanted my company after being put to bed. I learned at this milestone to enjoy, instead of dread, going to see my children late at night, because it was clear they were growing in these moments. I started to view going to see them at night as an exciting treat: to find out in what way they were growing. At this milestone, my son started to ask me questions like, "What can we do to make the baby [his newborn younger sister] happy?" Then he would answer his own question, "I'm thinking … what about … a bottle!" This was amazingly significant first because he was solving a problem and second because he was able to tell me that what he was doing was "thinking."

I noticed my daughter would put on a play where one doll helped another doll. I noticed this with my son too, although at a just slightly older age, but, these skills develop on their own timeline. In this way, where children repeatedly show concern for other human beings and their needs, this milestone shows growing empathy, or at least, a concern for other's problems, which had appeared in the previous milestone but in a subtler form. Note that expecting children to show true and genuine empathy before this is unrealistic. They won't know they hurt someone else or show remorse.

Dr. Brazelton describes this about children at the 3-year-old checkup (which means it appears somewhere between two and three years old):

> With all this bubbling imagination, two new attributes appear. A sense of humor is likely to surface, and a child's ability to show empathy for others will become apparent. When a baby cries, she may want to go to it. When another child is hurt, she will watch him carefully to see how he handles it, and she may even show sympathy for his pain. (ch. 13)

Feedback

Hailey has such a great imagination. She will watch something on TV and then later at bedtime will tell me a bedtime story with what she saw on TV. We built a tent fort and I was having trouble getting the blanket to stay up. Hailey moved the chair closer so that the tent would not fall down as much. – Christina

They are just great! So informative and very true to what's going on with my kid to a T! – Katie Blogg, about Toddler Milestones 9 and 10

Conflict Resolution

The child becomes so extraordinarily demanding at this milestone that you may start to explore some firmer approaches. For instance, once my daughter demanded I go to the grocery store right that second. She often wanted me to drop everything I was doing to be with her. She insisted on getting her own way, such as keeping her shoes on, even though they might be causing a health problem. With both of my older children, I found having some resistance to what was being asked of me was necessary, even though up until this age, I primarily used a tactic to at least indulge their need in fantasy. Let me be blunt: Their demands will be so high and so irrational that you may become out of control. Figuring out how you want to say "No" is something worth getting good at.

Both of my older children would relent at times during this period after I told them I expected them to do or not do something. (This is perhaps because of their growing concern for others.) With my first child, I was sterner, perhaps telling him forcefully, "I expect you to …" This was probably unnecessary. By the time my second child had reached this milestone, I had read the advice from Dr. Tsabary to have better conscious awareness of my emotions. Her book, *The Awakened Family*, gave me great insight into how to contain any anger or irritation I had as a mother. She advocates to simply identify the emotion you are feeling in heated moments and doing this can help you handle situations in a more responsible manner. During periods like this, the phrase "be firm but kind" ran through my mind. It's perfectly acceptable to turn down requests from your toddler that you don't want to satisfy. It is also acceptable to ask them to do certain things, like cut their nails. A confident, assured, and calm approach works well when asking children to cooperate with you. Assume success is likely! Sending you confidence, trust, and patience at this milestone.

What continued to work well for us was to give the child a choice where inaction was not a choice. You might say, "We are leaving now. You can choose to walk or I'll carry you." Almost 100% of the time, my children chose to walk, forgetting what they were just complaining about.

You can invite children into the problem-solving process starting at this milestone. You have to help them a lot at first. But you can for instance give several choices to solve a problem and then ask the open-ended question, "What do you think is a good solution?" You planted the idea of the solution, but they get their first experience in solving a problem as related to conflict resolution on their own. Here is an example of that, which is from my Facebook page, The Observant Mom:

> I was vacuuming, and my son always follows me around with a red car that he has when I do this, but his red car was missing. This is meltdown material. I decided to try this "problem-solving" method. I said, "We have a problem. The red car is missing. We could continue to look for it, use a different car, or think of another solution. What do you think a good solution is?" He thought for a moment and said, "I know! Let's use the blue car!" It was the first, and I think the very earliest time, this parenting tactic could have worked.

Activities

Talk about the events of the day at night during the bedtime routine.

Hang phonetic words next to their picture for the child to try to read.

Put Words Next to their Picture

I noticed my daughter kept trying to read words she saw, but the problem is that none of them were phonetic. I mean "June" or "CVS." Thanks, English language!

I put up the word "cat" with a picture of a cat at her bed.

At first, she would read it and say, "C. A. T. ... Ant!" I did not correct her (mistakes are also growth!), and it did not make much time for her to sound out each letter and say, "CAT!" and point to the cat. Then she rattled off several words that she knew from memory, sounding them out first and saying them. I was glad I had not corrected her, because when she did get it, I knew she *actually* got it and was not just copying me.

Toddler Milestone 10 – Abstract Reasoning

Starts: 2 Years, 8 Months, 3 Weeks
Most Intense: 2 years, 9 months
Ends: 2 years, 9 months, 2 weeks
Irritable Period Summary

Stalls at bedtime

Bossy about how routines are executed, e.g., agrees to do something but insist on doing something else first

Cries easily

Possessive of primary caregiver

Blocks people from moving

Most Intense Period

Cries, blocks caregiver from moving

New Abilities Summary

Distinctive

Can notice a pattern between things even if they aren't immediately in their sight, e.g., while looking at a tomato says it looks like an apple

Follows and commits to more longer-term verbal instructions better, e.g., "The safe spot is the side walk. Please stand there" or follows instructions in a class better

Impressive increase in imagination

Clever in figuring out how to get their own way, e.g., if they get to use a phone after a bath, they ask to take a bath often

Variable

Negotiate with you on their behalf

Sensitive to what you think of them

Demonstrate that they do not want to hurt someone else

Ask "Why?" often

Irritable Period Description

Just shy of 2 years, 9 months, another irritable period starts. My daughter would cry easily, get very possessive, and especially stalled performing her normal bedtime routine such that it dragged on longer.

One behavior that can be especially annoying is that she would block me from going places. This dissipated around 2 years, 9 months, 2 weeks.

New Abilities Description

What is most striking about this milestone is an ability to hold information in their head mentally and deal with it. A simple example is an ability to see a pattern between things even though they are not both in sight. My daughter once looked at a tomato and said, "Hi tomato, you look like an apple," and the apple was not in sight. She also put on a play with a potato asking if it was a potato or an avocado.

I could ask my daughter to do something and she would adhere to it more persistently. I was able to reliably ask her, for instance, to go stand on a sidewalk, a place we called the "safe spot" while I got the rest of what I needed out of our vehicle.

She became very clever. For instance, my daughter knew that she got to watch videos on my phone after she was finished with her bath. She would ask to take a bath to get the phone. Or, at night, she figured out if she did not drink her milk while we read books, she could drink milk after reading books, and then have more time with me. She negotiated with her dad about how long it would take to make bacon once. He told her it would take seven minutes. She argued, "No, one minute!" This is really a fascinating new skill. Children can hold an idea in their heads now for days and use it to make decisions. She also showed she could deal abstractly with the idea that seven is bigger than one.

I found my daughter was very sensitive to what I thought of her. She would color something and come up to me, nervously and excitedly, to see what I thought of it. In this, it may be a beginning idea of right and wrong. She was asking, "Am I right?"

She also showed that she did not want to see her brother hurt. Once they were fighting over if he could do a puzzle with her. She had it first, so I had to ask him to let her do it. He went to a corner and cried. My daughter said, "I want him to do the puzzle, because I don't want him to be sad." I am not sure if she experienced guilt, where she felt she caused the harm and felt bad, but she did recognize another person's pain and wanted to relieve it. I think, however, the very beginning feelings of guilt may be present during this milestone.

Feedback

Hailey has been reminding us of her birthday coming up. She can recall when her birthday is. She also tells us that she wants a Moana party. I have tried to convince her to go on a trip instead, but she is insistent that she wants a Moana-themed birthday party. She must've overheard her father and I talking about how much it would cost to get Moana to come to her party that she even asked her Nana for $200 for her birthday.

I will also add for [Toddler Milestone 10], Hailey has been going to dance class since she was 18 months old. It was so hard to control her in class because she would just run around and not follow instructions 100% of the time. Now she is the leader of the class and sets the best example. – Christina

[Milestone 10] for us this was the "I want mummy" leap. Max wanted me to do EVERYTHING and became super upset if for some reason I couldn't (and even more so if that reason had to do with our 4-month-old). He's become a lot more creative and his imaginative play is off the charts. Language has gone up a notch and I'm loving the conversations we're having now. Yesterday he put a dinosaur up his shirt and was talking quietly to himself about it being born as he pulled it out from under his shirt. Amazing! – Beck Fredrickson

Conflict Resolution

My primary tool during this milestone remained, "giving choice where inaction is not a choice." For instance, if they are refusing to go to bed, you can say, "You can come to me or I will pick you up." It acts as a warning, gives them some choice, and my experience is they usually choose the option where they have some control over the next course of action.

I sometimes gave a choice not related to what was going on. I did a joke with my daughter whereby, instead of getting her "fair and square," I caught her "fair and circle" or "fair and triangle." Before a diaper change, I might say, "Do you want me to catch you 'fair and circle' or 'fair and triangle'?" She would make her choice of the two and cooperatively go with me to change her diaper. This approach is better than yelling, hitting, or grabbing a resistant child.

When they become so very sensitive to what others think of them, descriptive praise is imperative. This is a skill for a parent to develop, where you actively take an interest in what your child creates, notice details about it, and give compliments.

Activities

Build a Model Neighborhood

My favorite activity at this milestone is to print out a map and then build a model of a place that the child frequents often, for instance, a model of your neighborhood. Then, using small figurines, mimic walking to the pool or park in your model neighborhood. If you followed the activities in Toddler Milestone 7 "Deliberate Rearranging and Creation," children will be already familiar with doing an activity where something is built from a set of instructions or a pattern, in the way that a model neighborhood is being built from a map in this activity. The difference now is that the child can remember the model that they built and, so, as they go outside on their next trip in the real neighborhood, they can mentally relate it back to the model they built. My daughter showed she understood the connections between the model and real life. This is an important conceptual level skill that you can build. You can also stress safely crossing streets or other issues as you walk around your model neighborhood.

Follow Me Games

To practice following instructions, you can play games where children have to follow instructions. An example is "Simon Says." At this young age, you might just have them copy your actions instead of getting penalized if they do the action if you don't say "Simon Says."

Another idea is to do "circle time" routinely. After a particular cue, such as the lights are dimmed or music is on, the child comes to an area in anticipation of a lesson or a book.

Toddler Milestone 11 – Budding Morality

Starts: 2 Years, 9 Months, 3 Weeks
Most Intense: 2 years, 10 months
Ends: 2 years, 10 months, 2 weeks
Irritable Period Summary

Whiny

Possessive of primary caregiver

In seeming disbelief of what is in front of their eyes, e.g., complain that butter is not on bread when it is

A large time delay in responding to real events, e.g., after their heads get stuck in a shirt, several seconds after they are no longer stuck, they break out into tears about it

Want all toys and food for themselves

Want to stay up late

Strong desire to do things themselves, resulting in meltdowns if they can't accomplish the activity / task

Extreme, major meltdowns, probably in public

Bossy to others about their role as they solve a problem they are working on

Does not handle change well, even immediate change, such as moving a utensil

Uncoordinated and clumsy

Most Intense Period

One or more terrible meltdowns where they seem confused and in disbelief of what is happening and where they boss you around a lot

New Abilities Summary
Distinctive

Evaluate courses of action as right or wrong based on time to apply the action, harm done, or what is ideal behavior, e.g., showing dad a picture they drew when dad gets home, trying not to spill the milk while carrying it, not hitting because it hurts

Fully understand short-term future plans and make their desired roles in those plans known, ask about what the plans are, tell others where they should be in those plans

State their strong likes and dislikes

State what a favorite thing of theirs is

Variable

Understand something in a process even though it goes out of sight, e.g., food goes into your belly

Vivid imagination, make up simple stories, e.g., person at the door "might be a monster"

Can be involved in planning activities, e.g., bedtime routine

Can count up to 30

Irritable Period Description

This milestone is terrible. My daughter became extraordinarily possessive of everything, from everyday objects to me, her mother. She had meltdowns easily and whined a lot. She was fearful that her needs wouldn't be met. She moved from, "I want to go over there," to crying hysterically that she wasn't where she wanted to be within seconds. She had a striking desire for independence and had a meltdown when things didn't go her way in moving towards a goal. She was very bossy in telling others what their role was in attaining her goal. There seemed to be a major time delay/confusion in how she responded to events. If you think of the brain like software code, it is as if the child's brain is trying to execute code that is broken and is stuck in an endless loop. My daughter once got her head stuck in a shirt and though she had got unstuck, several seconds later she burst into tears about it. She also seemed to be in disbelief of what was in front of her own eyes. It is best explained by one of the worst meltdowns we had, from my personal notes at 2 years, 10 months on the dot:

Tonight was a hell of a night. We went out to eat. Emily is clearly in an irritable period of a growth period and was, um, difficult. It started when the bread came out. At first, we had bread, but no plates. She was flipping out about this. We tried to tell her we were going as fast as we could and we had to ask the waitress. I invited her to help ask the waitress. She liked this, though she did not ask when we prompted her to. So, I did.

So the plates come out and the waitress was there. Emily was flipping out because she wanted not just bread, but butter too, and we later found out, to spread her own butter. Somewhere in there, the waitress started taking orders and Emily got a knife, which she grabbed by the blade. I pried her hands off, gently, and she started *screaming*. I was embarrassed, picked her up, and took her outside.

This helped nothing. I learned later that my two boys, who were otherwise calm the whole time, started crying. Emily never calmed down outside. She wanted the knife and to spread her own butter. She was distraught and no attempts to calm her down were helping. I was not able to explain the situation about having her hands on the blade of the knife (which actually didn't hurt her at all; and she has used many knives before this well). So, I had no choice but to bring a crying toddler back in. She was calmer but the bread, her bread, had been eaten by her brothers, who had been crying for it.

We got more bread; somehow she tolerated the three or four minutes it took. I ended up giving her the knife, and she spread the butter successfully. She spread her arms out, yelling, loudly, "I DID IT!"

It became a spread the butter nightmare after this. She would demand I hold the knife, and I wasn't allowed to put it down. The most interesting part, was that she would be screaming about something, that she wanted something, even though she already had it. So, she might scream, "I want butter on the bread," but the butter was on the bread. We had pulled out a Kindle Fire, which was no use really, and she would totally flip out that she thought someone was going to stop the movie, when the movie was still playing.

So, dessert comes out. (Because of several mistakes throughout dinner, they offered us free dessert. I think they may have taken pity on us.) We were at a table that was in the shape of a circle. We put dessert in the middle, but the kids were far away from it in their seats. Emily climbed up to get it and in doing this, pushed her chair back, which probably had butter all over it, and falls, splat on the floor. A total full body spill. Everyone looked at us. I picked her up and just held her. The manager offered more ice cream. My husband had then split the ice cream into bowls, which made Emily flip out. John (my oldest) started flipping out, because Emily wanted every bowl. I asked John if we could get ice cream on the way home for him and he agreed. Whew.

That night, I went home and sat with her well into the night. She showed off impressive counting and reading ability, talked about the day with me, and at times just burst into tears. I felt even more connected with her. After this, I started to see irritable periods as love opportunities. I believe this behavior should be seen as a Bat-Signal for us that children *need* us.

New Abilities Description

There is an impressive explosion of abilities at this milestone, qualifying it as a major one in my opinion, with major paradigm shifts.

In the last milestone, the child can hold on to ideas mentally for longer periods of time and use those ideas to compare ideas and act on those ideas reliably. This core skill of dealing with ideas mentally greatly expands. It can be hard to tell where the last milestone ended and this one begins, but, as one example, when we went to a cave on vacation once, before we went down into the cave, my daughter had seen candies in the shapes of crystals. At the end of the tour, she said, "Now we can go get candy!?" She had to remember this idea of the candies being there, remember it throughout the entire 90-minute tour, then upon the completion, know that this was a realistic time to go get the candy she wanted. When we were stalled on the tour of the cave, she asked questions like, "Is it time to go?" She was very aware of all plans being made and who was doing what and made her opinion known as to where she wanted to be in those plans. This is the seeming dominant new skill.

She also said things like "I don't want to spill it" if she was holding something that she might spill. In other words, "I want to do what's right." She could evaluate an action and see if the action should be applied or not. She knew that that buying candy is something she wanted to do, but it only makes sense to apply it after the tour was over when we were near the store that sold it. She did this without even seeing the store. Similarly, with holding the glass, she could evaluate that spilling it would be an undesirable course of action. She became into "rules" too, like "No taking!" She made her opinion known, strongly, of what rules others were to follow around her. This is why I named this milestone "Budding Morality."

Similar to evaluating right and wrong, she expressed strong likes and dislikes. My daughter once told me what her favorite things were (her lovie and blanket) and then broke out into "My Favorite Things" as sung by Julie Andrews in *The Sound of Music*. She asked me often if I liked the food I was eating. What other people liked/didn't like became very interesting to her.

Her imagination clearly grew, which is another example of how well children's ability to "see what isn't in sight" is growing. My daughter once heard someone wiggle her door knob and made up a dramatic, fun story that it "might be a monster!!" (Other mothers report this increase in imagination at the last milestone.) My children loved stories such as *The Three Little Pigs* or *The Gingerbread Man*. My son also made up a play. It was about how a train was being a good helper to help another train. Here is seen imagination, and also the issue of right and wrong, where the helper train performed rightly to save the train in distress. I noticed that this play was about something we praised him about, indeed telling him he was a "good helper." Both of my children took pride in being "good helpers" at this milestone and older.

My daughter was also capable of understanding where something goes in a process even though she couldn't see it. She would eat something and ask, "Where did the food go? In my belly?" An ability to deal with abstract thoughts like this, which are not in immediate sight, simply bursts at this age.

As a light of hope for what is this terrible, awful milestone: In the brief calm period before the next milestone, I found my daughter became very helpful. Her older brother once took a spill on a bike. Upon seeing this, she took the initiative to go over and help him up.

Feedback

We are definitely in [Milestone 11]! This is hell. Lol. She is whiney, crying, tantrum central. She has been screaming at the top of her lungs out of nowhere and will scream "NO!" Waking up in the middle of the night and is VERY clingy! Very strong opinions and a big imagination. When something is missing and I ask her where she put it, she tells me, "Maybe the neighbors took it." She knows she is having a bday party coming up. We are celebrating early and she keeps talking about her Moana party. – Christina, about her daughter Hailey

[Milestone 11] has become ridiculous. I cannot even with this child. He is mean, aggressive, screaming constantly. I feel like he is in a permanent meltdown. I've never seen him so unhinged. Please tell me it stops soon. He's 2y10m8d from EDD and 2y10m1d from his birthday. – Kate Mishriki Baglivo

Conflict Resolution

Giving limited choice starts to not "work" as well as previously. One night I asked my daughter if she wanted mommy or daddy to brush her teeth. She said, "Emily," meaning, she wanted to do it herself. She saw outside the paradigm, which was great insight into her forming mind. She knew what she wanted and where she wanted to be in plans, picked a choice not presented to her (not in immediate sight), and made her opinion quite known.

Given children's desire to move towards a goal, but total emotional meltdowns in trying at this milestone, it becomes imperative to speak the language of "emotions," especially during the irritable period. The natural reaction is going to be to show the children that they or you are working towards the goal. For instance, if they are watching a movie, they might become upset if they think someone who is adjusting the volume is instead trying to turn the movie off. You can say, "The movie is on dear! No one is turning it off!" but only say it once. Anything after this is nagging and lecturing. Speak to their emotions: "You're worried someone will turn the movie off?"

I found children want to get into seemingly everything at this age, and they aren't at all careful about how they go about things. Warn every adult in your house now that leaving anything out that you don't want a destructive toddler to get ahold of is equivalent to an act of high treason. Take notice of any beauty products that the child might get, medicine, knives, etc. You might leave these up high until the calm period of Toddler Milestone 12 (the next one).

The most powerful, and only thing really, that seemed to "work" to calm children down at this difficult milestone is to let them immerse themselves in their favorite activity. My son loved to build train tracks, and I think this helped calm him down a lot. I did not notice the terribleness of this milestone nearly as much with him as I did with my daughter. I couldn't find anything equivalent for my daughter as everything she wanted to do, such as paint, was very messy.

Children may become very accident prone or even possibly destructive, and I encourage you to think about how you might handle it. They are very perceptive to issues of right and wrong, so modeling calm and patient behavior becomes imperative, especially during a trying time. I used "storytelling" often during this milestone to postprocess some of the almost guaranteed accidents or traumas that happen. After a traumatic event, you tell the story, over and over, slowly at first, until it becomes just a past memory. Because children can remember past events so well now (from previous milestones) and have so many traumatic events during the irritable period of this milestone, you might find this tool handy. It can help you as the parent process them too. It helps to reflect on what happened and what healthy habits and approaches were when dealing with the event. Here is an example of that with one of the most popular stories that I have ever told on my Facebook page, The Observant Mom:

My daughter, 2 1/2, dropped a smoothie in a tall glass cup, which shattered on our rug. It was all I could do to remember the Dr. Ginott advice of, "The milk spilled, let's get a rag." I admit my initial, blind reaction was an exasperated, "Emily!" I immediately moved to start calming myself down, but I admit thinking, "Ok, the smoothie is all over the rug as well as splinters of glass, let's get a rag" was a bit overwhelming. I admit further I had a salacious desire to yell, "What's wrong with you?" I did *not* do this. I write about this kind of thing to let other parents know that others have this reaction too, to give some tools to deal with it, and to maybe prepare your heart for the next time you deal with it.

The advice that helps me the most is that of Dr. Tsabary to keep conscious tab of your emotions. I did that. I was fully aware and present with my negative emotion. It's hard. I remember almost this exact situation with my first child, when he was almost this exact age, when he spilled coffee on my laptop, then kept hitting his sister. Incidents like this caused me to look for tools for better emotional regulation. At the time, I tried using a timer to tell myself I wasn't allowed to respond until the timer was done. The timer kept getting lost. A real deep breath and being present with my emotions have been the most powerful tools I've found to date.

I did go to clean up the mess. I was thinking, "Oh my! And we are *not* getting another smoothie after this! No way!" That was my *thought*; it was not what I said. I even wanted to yell, "There is glass everywhere! Stay away!" I did not say this either. The truth is most glass was picked up and saying that was less concern for the child and more my exasperation.

I got a paper towel and a bag to clean it up. As I cleaned it up, and moved towards the solution, I calmed down greatly. My daughter came over and said, "I'll help you fix it!" I realized in this moment what a learning experience this was. This really is not just a matter of one incident; this stuff shapes the character of children and how they will handle these sticky moments in the future. Like Dr. Siegel writes in *The Whole-Brain Child*, moments like this allow you to thrive instead of just survive, if handled right. I did point out to her that a mess was made and that we were cleaning it up. I didn't do this to show her she was "wrong," but that her actions did cause a mess, and, accident or not, we move to repair any damage we cause.

I kept calming down and calming down. I remembered the advice in one of the *Positive Discipline* books about how "Try Again" is a magical phrase for a child. Maybe I could make another smoothie.

I did make another smoothie. I thought about saying, "And be careful!" I know better. This is not a good thing to say. Instead, as I went to make the smoothie, I said, "We'll try the smoothie again." This is a much better thing to say. It doesn't assume the child is a screw up like "Be careful" does and instead infuses confidence into the child. When I handed the second smoothie to my daughter, she said, "I don't want to spill it!" She already *knows* it was a problem. It's already "in" them to want to be respectful. We don't have to rub their noses in their mistakes.

Afterwards, we talked about the incident. I also learned this from *The Whole-Brain Child* by Dr. Siegel. He writes to do this for traumatic events. You tell the story over and over, slowly at first, until it is processed and becomes just a past memory. I use it often, whenever anything like this happens. My daughter keeps asking and talking about how the smoothie spilled, and we keep talking about how it was a mistake, but we moved to fix it, and I give her a high five and thank her for helping me.

As some inspiration, I will tell you that at slightly older than three years old, I found that when my daughter made a mistake, she would often say, "Let's try again!" How you react to these situations is so important. Letting your children know that mistakes are just mistakes can help build a foundation of resilience in them.

Talking about the day at the end of every night is a great nightly ritual to start now. They can remember the events of the day, though they are likely to confuse what happened today versus yesterday or even weeks prior. I also liked to do a "Happy/Sad" part of the day starting now. The child may or may not be able to answer this now, but they certainly like hearing which parts were "happy" and which ones were "sad." I found these late-night conversations were wonderful for getting to know what my child was thinking, in a calm setting.

Given children can talk and think about more long-term abstract ideas, they can be involved in planning. Now is a great time to establish formal routines. We made a bedtime routine describing what few steps there would be at every bedtime. The steps were printed out and put on my children's wall. I made sure to include the happy/sad part of the day on the routine, so they knew they would get this special time with me before bed. You could take a picture of your child doing each activity and put the pictures up as a fun alternative, taking advantage of almost literal mirror neurons. Your child might not adhere to the routine very well at this age, but it may help, and in a few months, they will get really good at following the routine.

Given their awareness of right and wrong and of short-term future plans, one of my favorite phrases was "Try Again." When they did something abusive with a toy, I would usually give a warning but if they did the action again, I would take the toy. I would say "We'll try again," and give the toy back within about one minute. If they were hitting a sibling with it, I put the toy away for a whole day out of respect for the other sibling. And, honestly, even giving a warning is probably unnecessary. It is OK to follow up with swift action by taking the toy and giving it back within a minute with the confidence-building, "We'll try again now." Act, don't talk.

It is important to continue to give descriptive praise for ideal actions and clear guidance and information about undesirable actions. Children are clearly capable and make their desire to know right from wrong known. This will expand greatly in the next milestones.

I strongly favor using "I" statements" starting at this age. This is a way to set a clear expectation and takes advantage of the natural empathy in children. Here is an example of this at this milestone, with a story from my Facebook page, The Observant Mom:

I start using "I" statements with my children at very young ages. I use them at all ages, because I think they are the proper way to set boundaries, but I find the statements start to "work" with children who are in their very late twos. In my documentation on cognitive growth, children start to understand simple notions of right and wrong in an abstract way starting around 2 years, 10 months (and slightly earlier in a very subtle form). They go through a cognitive spurt at this time—a really irritating and frustrating one by the way. Using an "I" statement worked today for my daughter, 2 years, 10 ½ months:

She had food in her mouth and was playing this silly game where she bounced on my chest with her hands and back while showing me the food in her mouth. Whatever—she's 2, this is what she is interested in, and I try to respond to her, as I think it's a bid for connection. But when she bounced on me, she kept hitting my nipple. It hurt. I don't always respond in a calm way in these situations. Sometimes I respond with, "OW!" But I was in a rested and calm sitting position, and I was able to think in the split second that I needed to form a thought, and I said, "I see your food. But when you hit me right here [pointing to where it hurt] it hurts me." This is an "I" statement, with its three parts. I showed her what she was doing (bouncing), how I felt about it (it hurt) and why it upset me (it hurts).

She started bouncing on me with only one hand, such that her other hand did not touch me where I said it hurt!

They absolutely are capable of respecting your boundaries! I made the investment to use this type of boundary setting with my first son, who is now 5, and his ability to handle conflict resolution is impressive. It's a worthwhile language to learn. It can bring a lot of calm to your house—eventually. It's a process to get there, and one I try to put into place as early as possible.

However, giving information in an "I" statement like this doesn't always have the same effect. Children become much more strong-willed. They understand plans are being made, and they want to be part of them. If I gave information and they do not respond well, I still use "give choice where inaction isn't a choice."

And, Mom and Dad, I think you may need a break! This milestone and the next one are rough. Can you find a way that you can have some time for yourself or to get a date night? Please consider planning this now, before you get in over your head. To anyone who takes children off their parents' hands at this milestone, bless your soul. You are doing them a great favor.

If you cannot find extra help, please do what you can to increase your stock of patience and wisdom.

Activities

Involve Them in Cleaning or Other Household Activities

A great activity is to simply get them involved in some bigger and important things around the house, such as cleaning up the toy room. Give them praise when you see something they do nicely. For instance, "I saw how gently you put that toy away. Thank you." This gives you great practice at setting the expectations you have for them. At the end of clean up, I would also do an "inspection." I would walk around noticing how everything was put away, "I see how those wood blocks are put in their box," etc. My children loved this.

It is likely that they will want to be involved in cleaning, cooking, etc., and it can get out of hand quickly. My daughter grabbed knives by the blade, lipstick by the lipstick part, carried around drinks triumphantly (which spilled, often), and wanted to make coffee for me, resulting in the cream spilling everywhere. Being pro-active with lessons is necessary. It helps facilitate their growth too.

You can also notice what is unique about your child by doing an activity like this. In the example of cleaning the toy room, my son would build simple machines to put away toys, such as building a ramp to slide his toys up into a bin. My daughter showed impressive organizational ability and fine motor control. I learned not to correct how they did things or worry if they went very slowly but to just see it as a clue to their unique talents.

Three-Part Montessori Reading Lesson

For reading, in order to know that "dog" matches an actual dog, children need to be able to read "dog" and be able to conjure in their mind a picture of a dog. Therefore, the imagination seen at this milestone (and which probably starts in subtle form in the last milestone) is necessary for this step in reading. Doing a three-part Montessori reading lesson is a great activity to facilitate this, assuming the child can spell out a few simple words now. In the below picture, my daughter is matching the word (the first part) to the picture (the second part) and the answer key is sitting face down next to her activity (the third part).

I found that my daughter had trouble with the last letter of words. She once incorrectly did "map" and "mat," which revealed that she was spinning off the first letter. To give her an assist with this, I did at first three sets of three words as follows: "hat, cat, mat"; "man, can, fan"; "sad, mad, glad." I did one set per day. This gave her experience with these words and then I did "mat, man, mad" to give practice selecting the last letter correctly. She was able to do this "mat, man, mad" lesson in her early threes.

If you do this activity for the next several years, of simply putting a word next to its picture or on an object, you do your child a great favor. My son learned to read this way easily, and he found great joy in being able to figure out how to read new words based on the context clues, such as road signs or restaurant signs. Many educational apps, videos, and books provide pictures with words next to them. This is the easiest and most joyful way to learn how to read.

Beginner Books

Any beginner book can be used. I made a big mistake with my first child by demanding he read the words without much assistance from me. I changed my approach with him, and it was for the better. I had previously thought that if I read the book to him, he would memorize it, and then the educational value would be lost as he wouldn't be sounding out the words. How wrong I was! My approach to beginner books is to read them with your children as often as they want and for fun. Then we talk about the pictures to understand the story better. I also act out the book as a play on occasion. Make it fun! Many beginner books list the new words at the beginning of the book. If so, we talk about the words at the beginning. I don't make my children sound out the words. I point to the word and say what it is. The whole lesson should be fun and easy for both you and your child. I found my daughter would sometimes figure out words on her own. She once looked at words, and I could tell she was deep in thought, and she then, pointing correctly to the words, read the sentence, "Bob hits the tin can."

Tying Numerals to Number of Objects

An activity to tie together the abstract symbol of a number (the numeral) and the actual number is ideal at this milestone. Print them out and lay them on a set of stairs. This is an easy and fun way for children to learn the concept of zero, as you start at "0" and must actively go up one stair to get to "1."

Count to 100

    I noticed my daughter could count up to around the number 30 or 40 on her own. This was learned largely by the calendar she had by her bed. We counted off the days each night, starting from 1. She once counted the cracks in a sidewalk up to 39 and then got stuck at what comes after that. To clear up this confusion, I simply put Unifix Cubes in groups of 10 by color and laid the numeral by 10 out. The result is one long rod that goes to 100, with 10 colors of 10 cubes each. It is quite the accomplishment to get to *"one hundred!"*

    Another way to do this is to use a Rekenrek. This is like an Abacus where there are 10 beads hanging on each rod, with 10 rods for a total of 100 beads. However, the beads on the Rekenrek are colored such that there five beads colored one color and five beads colored another on each rod. It is very similar to the beads used in a Montessori classroom, but they are integrated into one manipulative, which is usually less expensive and will take up less room in your house. You can count the beads with your child. It easily shows that you count to 10 and then on the next rod, you slide one more over such that $10 + 1$ is 11. This is a great math manipulative for later lessons on adding, subtracting, and skip counting as well.

    I spent a lot of time trying to get my first child to count past 100 when he was between the ages of 3 and 5. I had some successes. However, I found at a milestone which I have tentatively documented at 5 years, 2 months called "Algebraic Thought," my son became extremely interested in large numbers. (He became interested in how big or small things got often as a continuum, hence the name "Algebraic Thought.") If I could do it over again, I wouldn't have worried about counting past 100 until that milestone, when the child becomes absolutely fascinated with how big or how small things can be. At these ages, the toddler and preschool years, spending time here with numbers between 0 and 100 and having fun with them is a great way to approach numbers.

Put on a Play

I put on plays all throughout toddlerhood (and older!) but how we used them changed. At this age, children can remember the entire story and might even take over the process and put the whole thing on themselves. They can understand some of the simple themes of the story as well. They can project what they want to do into the future and can follow the steps to get there so well that a play is a perfect activity. This is a great activity to build reading comprehension. Some favorites for my children were *Cinderella, The Gingerbread Man, The Three Little Pigs*, and *The Great Pie Robbery* by Richard Scarry.

Toddler Milestone 12 – Budding Integrity

Starts: 2 Years, 11 months
Most Intense: 2 Years, 11 Months
Ends: 3 years
Irritable Period Summary

Want a lot of attention

Whiny

Meltdowns

Won't let you leave at bedtime

Stall at bedtime, might say they have to go potty or say they are hungry (but they don't eat much when you get them food)

Want to be "in" everything, such as medicine and such that they shouldn't be in

Want to "help" do everything

Attached to your leg

Won't accept "No" as an answer

Become back-seat drivers, dictating what street they want you to go down

Plays with picking the wrong tool for a job, e.g., brushes hair with a book

Most Intense Period

The intense part starts off right away with a lot of spills, accidents, and whining. They also may demand to stay up really late. However, it gets a lot better over the next few weeks

New Abilities Summary
Distinctive

Understand directions of how to get around, such as how to get around a relatively new place, such as a new restaurant, or how to get somewhere familiar by car

Say "I'm sorry" and "You're welcome"

Accepting of "No" as an answer

Is much more willing to adhere to requests, even if against their own whim at the time, e.g., please don't get into a pool that you are filling up with water

Better emotional control, collect themselves after they fall

Noticeable better control over their body, don't fall as much

Variable

Better at playing cooperative games where players take turns

Put on plays of their own design

Interested in small details

Squint their eyes and points to things

Irritable Period Description

This irritable period starts with a bang. It doesn't crescendo as some of the others do. It isn't terribly rough, at least not as rough as the overall irritable period of Toddler Milestone 11, but coming off of Toddler Milestone 11, I personally felt burned out, and it was difficult to deal with yet another one. As such, the start of this one marked what I consider to be the most difficult time during the entire toddler years. I found my daughter demanded my attention a lot and wanted to help with everything I was doing. I often couldn't move an inch without bumping into her and I really had to struggle with her as to why she couldn't play with diaper paste or have prescription medicine. At its worst from my personal notes:

I am really struggling with Emily lately. She took a full-blown spill on our hard wood floors today, after running off with a tomato, biting into it, which caused the juice in the tomato to leak and make the floor slippery. She is attached to my leg seemingly at all time. When you can't open a door to get to the garbage can, go to the bathroom, change a diaper, etc., without a person right there blocking you, it can grate on you. I have to fight with her over why I might not want a vitamin at the moment she wants to give me one or why I can't let her put certain topical ointments on by herself. I can handle any of these things in isolation. Handling three or more highly irritating situations throughout the day and a bunch of little ones over the course of the day, from 9 am to 9 pm, can really wear on a person. I had to do a mom timeout tonight after she kept demanding my attention at night and wouldn't go to bed.

Thankfully, my husband took over and spent time with her.

Our daughter turned into a back-seat driver. She was insistent that the driver of the car we were riding in turn down a different road than the route we were on.

This irritable period seemed to dissipate greatly as it went on, but then got slightly worse before it completely dissipated at three years old.

Good news, however: many new skills emerge revealing a more mature child whom you can ask to do things and then does.

New Abilities Description

Depending on when you read this, you might not believe me, but the defiance found in the irritable period does melt away—if you let it melt away, by extending trust to the child.

I describe in the summary some of the skills seen. The first one I list is understanding navigational directions, because this is the most obvious skill you might see, and it explains the milestone so well. Children might know the turn by turn directions to get from their home to, say, the grocery store. There is a complex problem to solve in which there are different paths that can be taken to get to the store, and they delight in figuring out the right way to get there. This is the core of this milestone: Figuring out the right way, path, or function of something when multiple choices or paths are available.

At this milestone, I once made a smoothie with my daughter and she was insistent on figuring out how to make it properly, such as putting in the proper ingredients and putting on the lid on the blender. This is an eloquent example of this milestone: how the child tries to understand the function of something. The child rationally tries to do things right instead of simply being a force of entropy. Congratulations, Mom and Dad, you made it through the toddler years!

At this milestone, we once went to a restaurant. My daughter saw we were at a restaurant and said, "I want to eat and drink! I'm so hungry!" I went to offer her juice as we got out of the van. She didn't want it. I think she saw we were at the restaurant, knew that we eat and drink at a restaurant, and partook in the joy and understanding of that. Knowing this helped in many other parenting situations. She threw off her blanket once and said, "I'm so cold!" I went to get her blanket for her, but I realized she was simply matching her coldness to the use of the blanket. So, I just said, "Oh! Do you need your blanket!?"

At this milestone, my daughter became interested in picking the right tool for the job. She once got a fork and spoon out and said to them, "Fork or spoon? Which one should I use?" Similarly, she delighted in the book *Are You My Mother?* by P.D. Eastman. In this book, a bird goes on a journey to find who the bird's mother is: a kitten, hen, dog, cow? She loved this kind of, "Is this one right? No. Is this one? No. Is this one? *Yes!*" At Toddler Milestone 9 (2 years, 8 months), the child does start to match a solution to a problem. The difference in this milestone is the child delights in having *many* options to choose from and figuring out which one is best.

I debated what to call this milestone, but when I saw how easily and with understanding my daughter said, "I'm sorry" and "You're welcome," I decided to formally call it "Budding Integrity." Both of these statements acknowledge if you did something right or wrong. "I'm sorry" means you know the right way but you didn't do it; so you say, "I'm sorry." "You're welcome" means you know the right way and someone acknowledged it, and so you say, "You're welcome." This is very characteristic of this milestone, in which there is a right or wrong way, and the child tries to adhere to it (the definition of integrity).

My daughter became much better at responding to my requests or instructions. She did what was right regardless of what would seem like her own whim wanted. I once went to leave the house, and she was right at the door saying, "I'll help you!" Based on past experience, I thought she would want to run out the door with me and then get mad that I left after she did. When I finally just left, after unsuccessfully trying to get her away from the door, all she wanted to do was close the door behind me. At the grocery store, just weeks before this, it would have been a battle to get her to put whatever she was holding on the conveyor belt. She often got fruit and carried it around the store. At this milestone, on her own volition, she put a banana on the conveyor belt, with no prompting from me to do it. She knew this is what you do at the checkout.

My daughter became very thankful any time anybody did something for her. If she was trying to complete a set of instructions and if someone helped her do it, she was grateful. When she put the banana on the conveyor belt previously described, the cashier bagged it for her and handed it back to her. She said, "Thank you! Thank you so much!" During this milestone we visited the local botanical garden. She got a map of the gardens to use while we were there, but at some point during our visit, the map ripped. On our way out, she handed the map to the person who gave it to her and then stood, waiting. He gave her a new map. She said, "Thank you for giving me the map! Thank you so much!" I include this for anyone worried that the child's bossiness in the irritable period is something to worry about it. It's not. It quickly melts away to reveal a child with enormous gratitude.

She showed she had a lot more emotional control in general. If she fell and took a spill on the floor, she could collect herself better and not break out into tears as quickly. What a relief!

This is from a *Wall Street Journal* article about a book by Erica Komisar entitled *Being There: Why Prioritizing Motherhood in the First Three Years Matters*. I include it for the insight about the child's ability to regulate emotions by the time they are three years of age:

"Babies are much more neurologically fragile than we've ever understood," Ms. Komisar says. She cites the view of one neuroscientist, Nim Tottenham of Columbia University, "that babies are born without a central nervous system" and "mothers are the central nervous system to babies," especially for the first nine months after birth.

What does that mean? "Every time a mother comforts a baby in distress, she's actually regulating that baby's emotions from the outside in. After three years, the baby internalizes that ability to regulate their emotions, but not until then." For that reason, mothers "need to be there as much as possible, both physically and emotionally, for children in the first 1,000 days." (Taranto)

My daughter absolutely loved putting on plays. She could put on the entire play almost by herself. One of her favorites was *The Gingerbread Man*. A "little old lady" puts a gingerbread man in the oven and he pops up and runs away, taunting, "Run, run as fast as you can, you can't catch me, I'm The Gingerbread Man!" My daughter could put on this play (and others) by herself and she delighted in pretending to be The Gingerbread Man. With as much as they like to play with getting around, I think the fun of running away to wherever she wanted after hopping out of the "oven" was much in alignment with her new interests and abilities.

I found both my son and daughter taking an interest in some of the small details of, say, books. When I put on a Cinderella play with my son, he remembered where the cat should be in certain scenes. My daughter took an interest in small details like this, indeed also mice/rats, in the books we read. If something spilled, even the smallest little speck of something, she would insist it be cleaned up.

At this milestone, my daughter squinted her eyes a lot. It seemed like she was closing one eye to focus on something far away and often pointed to it. I am not sure the cognitive significance of this, but it is worthy of noting. Cognitive growth spurts involve the child developing a new perceptual awareness so that the fact of her focusing her eyes differently is relevant.

Feedback

We are definitely in [milestone 12]! It is worse than [11]!!! She has really discovered her "opinion." If I tell her no and she gets mad, she will slam doors. She also will shout, "I'm so mad!" when she is very upset. She has become "bossy" and will try to boss other kids around. On the plus side, she is able to follow instructions well enough where I don't need to be next to her every single minute. She is what we call our sour patch kid; first she's sour and then she's sweet. We took her to the pediatrician's office for some stomach issues and she was telling us to "sssshhh" like she was embarrassed we were talking about her poop issues. – Christina, mom of Hailey

[Milestone 12]????? She's 2 yrs 11 mo 4 days. We've had massive sleep disruptions, is this normal? She's definitely trying to stay up later and had dropped naps over 6 months ago. Now she's up at about 4 or 5 am and having to have the occasional nap. Which is ok if I manage to get it in at 11:30/12, but at 2:45; it makes bedtime a nightmare!!! […] We're also having massive meltdowns if she doesn't get something exactly as she wants it (but these are directly related to tired/hungry moments as well!). – Tara Watts

Conflict Resolution

At this milestone, I stopped using "give a choice where inaction is not a choice" as much. I still used it on occasion, but only as a last resort. Instead, I first appealed to my child's growing reasoning capability and sense of right and wrong and often in a playful way.

In *Between Parent and Child*, Dr. Ginott gives the advice to advise the child about the function of an object if they are using one improperly. This approach starts to work beautifully at this milestone. As an example, if the child is jumping on the couch say, "The couch is for sitting." Whenever I asked my daughter to do something and she did it, I often flattered her about what a great and important thing she did and that I was grateful. She once handed something to a waitress, and I trumpeted it. She buried her head into her dad's chest, in slightly embarrassed pride, exclaiming, "I did it!" This approach emphasizes what to do, instead of what not to do.

I played with "giving information" in a way that delighted my toddler at this milestone. Maria Montessori describes in *Montessori Elementary Materials* that it helps to teach something by removing it, to reveal its function better. When teaching grammar, she recommends occasionally removing the word from a sentence so you see its function.

188

"Run the room." This makes no sense, but "Run around the room" does. Montessori describes that this is similar to how a person who has a failed organ can help scientists learn the proper function of that organ. Remembering this, I often played with my toddler about the correct use of something. I once wanted her to put her plate on the table, and she was defiant. I put the plate on my head and asked, "Is this where plates go?" She enthusiastically replied, "No!" Then I did the same thing by putting the plate on the refrigerator, the kitchen counter, a column in our house, and finally the table. She delighted in sitting at the table with the plate.

This is a related story from my Facebook page, The Observant Mom, about helping my daughter come to a better decision using a comforting approach:

My daughter gets one vitamin per day. She knows this and usually follows it, but sometimes she wants to eat the whole jar of vitamins. At this milestone, she started to do that, by filling a cup up with vitamins, which she wanted to take to the couch to eat. I told her she needed to put the vitamins back. She didn't, and I took the cup from her, which made her mad. I gave the cup back, showing I trusted her. She was crying about it and I said, "You're worried I'll take the cup?" This validation of her fear seemed to calm her down. I picked out two vitamins and told her she had to pick one. She grabbed both, but did not eat either, and just looked at me a little defiantly, as if deep conflict and confusion. I continued to communicate through my body language that I trusted her by relaxing my shoulders and softening any tense facial expression I had. Knowing she loves to figure out how things work and be involved in somewhat lengthy processes, I offered to make frozen fruit popsicles with her. She delighted in this. Then she asked about the two vitamins I had handed her, "Which one should I eat? Number 1 or number 2?" I suggested number 1. She ate the one vitamin and then put the rest back! I could tell the whole time she was struggling to make the right decision, and by extending some trust and comfort to her, I was able to facilitate this. Comfort, not harshness, helps children make better decisions. It was a delight to make popsicles with her.

As another example of helping my daughter make a good decision: My daughter loved to play in a shallow pool. I asked her to not get in it, and then she did. Knowing she was struggling with right and wrong and having recently heard the advice to ask a child if they truly understood what you said, I asked, "Did you make the right choice or the wrong choice?" She gave me that cute look little kids give when they just got caught at something (a surprise face), paused, thought about it, and said, with a huge smile, "Um … I made the *happy* choice!"

I sometimes would play the "which way?" game with my daughter. If she wouldn't go to her room at bedtime, I would ask, singing, "Which way? Which way?" meaning, which way should we go to get to her bedroom. I also would give markers or objects for her to go find if she wouldn't cooperate when going somewhere. "See those red flowers over there? Go to them. Now see that statue? Go to it."

I did formal lessons at this milestone about ideal behavior. I did some where I put on a play about something that happened to my child. I found my children loved this type of lesson, where they are the star in the play of some conflict that created drama. From my Facebook page, The Observant Mom:

We've been dealing with my 2-year-old being two lately. I ask my children for their happiest and saddest part of the day at night. I am glad I do. It's been a gold mine to find out what they are really thinking. My son told me his sad part was how his sister lays on him sometimes. I thanked him for telling me, because when this happens, it looks like play to me. I made a promise to him to stop her if I see it. I've been itching to give her more formal lessons about ideal behavior, now that, in her late twos, I think she will respond well.

Today an opportunity presented itself. I had asked my kids to clean the toy room. I had put blue tape down and my son, 5, went to clean it up. My daughter, 2, got really mad at this. I asked my son to stop, and he did. He put his foot on the tape to smooth it out. His sister came over and pushed him. He went into the bathroom, seemingly sad.

I saw my opportunity. I've gotten a little better at making impromptu lessons like this. And it really is a "lesson." I drew out exactly what happened on the white board. As I did it, my son corrected me that he was not sad; he was confused. I thanked him for clarifying his emotion! My daughter, two, was enthralled by this. Both children wanted to hear the story over and over again. My daughter re-enacted it, but now playing the part of her brother. I concluded for her on the board, "No Hitting."

I don't know yet if this will have an impact. This happened today. But I can tell you she can repeat the story and repeat that,

"Hitting [her brother] made him sad." Lessons like this went a long way with our first child when he was three to four years old.

This is what I mean by cognitive milestones as "investment opportunities." I know that my daughter is starting to explore ideas of right and wrong. I invest in teaching ideal behavior to her when I notice she takes an interest. It is for her and our immediate and long-term benefit.

This milestone also needs to come with a big **warning** about locks. With as insistent and good at figuring out how things work, children may become interested in learning how to unlock a door. I have heard of so many three-year-olds escaping their houses, when their parents had no idea they could unlock a door and otherwise felt their child was safe. These new abilities happen suddenly and indeed take parents by surprise. If you don't have a lock that is out of the child's reach, do that now. A simple chain lock can be placed at the eye level of adults.

Activities

Any activity where the child can pick the right course of action or the right answer or the right tool for the job or be given a set of instructions to execute are great. Below are a few ideas.

Illustrate Familiar Car Rides

On car rides, draw your toddler's attention to the route we were taking. Count how many "STOP" signs you see or ask which way to turn. Draw a map out to get to a familiar place, say, the grocery store. Draw numbers on the map with a landmark to look for, such as a stop sign, water tower, or a gas station.

Google Maps

This is an app that you can get. You can show them your neighborhood and talk about the route you would take to get to a favorite or familiar place.

Cardinal Directions

This worked for us just slightly beyond this age, at just over three years old, but this is the first I think you can do an activity where you teach the cardinal directions (North, East, South, West). Simply put a compass on a driveway or sidewalk. With chalk, draw the four directions coming off of the compass. Then ask the child to walk in each direction. It should be fun and not forced. Then do this in a different spot. Then do it again on a different day. You emphasize in this way that these directions never change.

Let Them Explore in an Open Area

If you can go to a zoo or park and let them experiment with getting around, going the direction that they choose, they are sure to have fun with this. Be prepared they may want to go down unconventional paths. Avoid anything that might confuse them, for instance a corn maze in which their view is obstructed, as this could scare them.

Walk the Line

This is a Montessori activity. A line is created on the floor, say with tape, and the child walks on it like a balance beam. You can expand it to have different ways the child can go and has to pick a particular path. They can also push cars or trucks from one destination to another with the tape.

Mazes and Maps

You can create a maze or a map for the child to get through in many different ways. I would sometimes take wooden rods and arrange them as a "maze" to push toy cars through. A maze as found in a workbook may soon become fun and possible to the child. We had a mat with a map on it that we would play with sometimes.

Follow Me Games

Simple childhood games like Red Light/Green Light or Follow the Leader may be fun.

Learning Resources Code & Go Robot Mouse Activity Set

I only weakly recommend this toy for a child of this age. This toy is recommended for ages 5+ but I found my daughter could do it, in a limited way. It comes with green squares, walls, and tunnels that can be assembled to make a maze, with "cheese" at the end of the maze. A battery-powered mouse can be programmed to start at one end of the maze and go get the fake cheese. I gave my daughter great assists in showing her how to do it. I played with the idea of "Is this the right way? No. Is this? No. Is this? Yes," as I showed her how to interlock the green squares to make the area for the mouse. I started by going only one square to get the cheese, then two, then three, then added turns. This was after showing her how to clear out the previous program, enter a program, and hit go. It took several days of training, but she did get it.

Hex Bugs

Hex Bugs are the exact opposite of the Code & Go Mouse. They are battery-powered "bugs" that vibrate and move around a maze and go in any random direction. I at first strongly preferred the Code & Go Mouse, given it was goal-oriented, but I cannot deny how much my children loved seeing Hex Bugs or other similar toys. I have to think Hex Bugs, which are motorized anarchy, speak to something deep in a child at this age.

Train Tracks, Car Sets

There is no shortage of car sets with cars that go down ramps and such in toy stores. If your child builds train tracks on their own, they might start to show increasing ability in making tracks where decisions must be made. You can draw their awareness to this and give them a vocabulary of the need to make a "decision." If not interested in building them themselves, you might make one for them to push around and make decisions as to which way to go. You can also build models of real tracks, such as a model of real car racing tracks.

Involve Them in Chores

You probably won't be able to say no to a child. They will insist on helping with everything. It is likely in your interest to just let them.

Messy Fun or Sensory Bins

The child wants to be "in" everything at this milestone. It's as if they need to be immersed in things. You can (try) to redirect it with something like a sensory bin. Their attention span does increase, and this might hold their attention for some time—to give you a moment to breathe! You may need to wait until after the irritable period to try this. My children's favorite sensory bin was some type of "dirt" or sand with a set of toy trucks to dump, excavate, or bulldoze the sand.

Books

These are some books that may appeal to a child at this milestone. Anything that plays with finding the right (or wrong!) answer or driving somewhere are likely to be fun. These are just examples—many other books are likely to be a hit as well:

Are You My Mother? by P.D. Eastman. A baby bird isn't sure which animal is his mother.

Let's Go for a Drive by Mo Willems. Gerald and Piggie want to go on a drive until their plans are spoiled.

"That's Silly!" feature in the Highlights for Children magazine where you pick out something in the picture that is silly.

Play Music from Sheet Music

It may become possible for the child to follow along with color-coded notes and play them on, for instance, a color-coded xylophone.

Human Anatomy

My daughter spontaneously showed she understood that food goes into your "belly" and gets eliminated. Puzzles about human anatomy are one example of an activity, tracing where food goes through the body.

Children are likely to become interested in doctors' equipment (if they weren't already). A real stethoscope and otoscope are surprisingly inexpensive. My daughter absolutely loved to give and get pretend medical checkups. Doing this can help them prepare for their three-year checkup. You can also prepare for their likely first dentist visit at three years old by flashing a light in their mouths and counting their teeth.

Makeup and Dress Up

You could give them lipstick, chapstick, or blush, and let them put it on correctly. It takes some patience as they learn. I would recommend waiting until the calm period of this milestone to try this.

Your Child's Third Birthday

Happy birthday to your now preschooler!! An activity your child might like at his or her third birthday is helping bake their own cake.

Future Milestones

This is the conclusion of milestones that I documented for the toddler years. The future milestones your child will experience after the age of three until the age of five will be covered in my book on preschoolers. From my rough notes at the time that I write this, this inquisitive nature late in the toddler period into what is right or wrong and what is true or false marks much of the preschool years. In the preschool years, it expands greatly, with if/then logic, coming to conclusions based on limited evidence, and verifying, with their own eyes and/or experimentation to see if something is true or if something works. They play with both social and scientific principles. I consider all of this to be the growth of reasoning skills. Children love to experiment in the preschool years. Instead of calling what they do "testing," I am making a small effort to call it "experimenting." "Testing" usually means they are pushing the limits of authority. "Experimenting" lends itself to show how they are natural scientific explorers of the world. I found my first child absolutely loved to do science experiments during the preschool years. In the fours, they become fascinated with big picture history (e.g., space and dinosaurs) and big ideas of right and wrong, e.g., justice and punishment. These are exciting ages in which a child can be taught an impressive array of skills, especially emotional regulation and conflict resolution skills.

I found, however, during the preschool years, once they determine one way is the "right" way, they become rigid about it. This rigidity melts away at five years old, the first elementary aged milestone, which I tentatively name the milestone of "Negotiation and Reasonableness." Just a heads up of what you might be in for!

Future Study

I fully expect this body of knowledge to grow. I have worked with many other parents to amend or add to this knowledge. In all cases, it was an amicable process to discuss the differences in what we saw with our children to get to more detailed, more accurate observations. The research presented here has been kicked around, banged on, and used, but I still fully expect this research to grow. This should be its own body of science, and many scientists of various pursuits can contribute to it.

Going forward, it has been said before that it is difficult to study natural developmental stages of children over 18 months with behavior-based external observation alone, because culture seems to affect their behavior. I submit the argument that parenting style *does* matter when it comes to doing research: It matters, however, not so much because it alters the behavior of the child, but because certain parenting styles can confuse the results. The issue that matters the most is the use of punishment. A parent is most likely to start to use punishment when a child is 18 months old. From Dr. Brazelton's *Touchpoints—Birth to Three* about his experience with parents as a pediatrician at the 18-month checkup:

> Most pressing will be their [parents] concern about the toddler's increasing negativism. "She won't listen to me anymore! I don't want to spank her, but sometimes I don't know what else to do. She'll keep on pushing and pushing until I have to do something. Whenever she has a tantrum, she always seems to pick the most embarrassing spot." Mothers will get teary as they speak of the changes in the child. Fathers tend to raise the question of punishment. (ch. 11)

Punishment, as described in the introduction, creates secondary, negative reactions in a child. If children are under the care of austere parenting, they will show more irritable and defiant behavior. It thus becomes impossible to differentiate behavior that is a negative, reactionary response to the austere parenting, behavior that is part of natural development, or a mixture of both.

How a child is taken care of emotionally also matters. For instance, in *Parent Effectiveness Training*, Dr. Gordon writes, as a major advantage of his method, which is negotiation-based instead of authoritarian, that families who use it don't see much teenage rebellion, which was previously thought to be an inevitable stage. Dr. Gordon writes:

> I was sure that adolescence, as most studies have shown, was invariably a time of storm and stress in families. Our experience with P.E.T. has proven me wrong. Time and time again, parents trained in P.E.T. have reported the surprising absence of rebellion and turmoil in their families.
>
> I am now convinced that *adolescents do not rebel against parents.* They only rebel against certain destructive methods of discipline almost universally employed by parents. Turmoil and dissension in families can be the exception, not the rule, when parents learn to substitute a new method of resolving conflicts. (ch. 1)

I submit that future behavior-based study of natural childhood developmental stages must be conducted with children who are not subject to punitive parenting measures. I insist also that any comprehensive critical review of my research, from parents or researchers, also be compared only against children who have not been subject to punitive measures and who are in physically and emotionally comforting homes. I expect, also, as non-punitive, observant parenting approaches become more adopted, that more and more people will be able to add to this research.

I look forward to seeing what kind of inquiry this research might inspire. And, if you do further research about this based on this work, as a parent or researcher, contact me. I'd like to know about it!

###

Thank you, Reader!

Many thanks to you for choosing to read this book! My goal is to communicate knowledge about cognitive growth cycles, which is a part of the bigger effort to get away from telling children how they are wrong and instead to look for those subtle signs of what is right and let it shine. If you would like to spread the word about cognitive growth spurts, please consider recommending this book to a friend or consider writing a review of this book, *Misbehavior is Growth: An Observant Parent's Guide to the Toddler Years*, at your favorite retailer of books. Come join the discussion as well on the Facebook forum, "Misbehavior is Growth—The Discussion."

For updates on future work, including work I have already started for the preschool and elementary years, please come join me on Facebook at "The Observant Mom" and visit my website, www.TheObservantMom.com, which has free printouts of the summaries of each milestone.

Recommended Reading

Following are books I recommend for parents of toddlers and why I do so, grouped by topic.

Handling Your Emotions

The Awakened Family by Dr. Shefali Tsabary
If you have any problem containing your own anger, this is the book to read. Dr. Tsabary advocates an approach where you become more conscious of your own emotions, which I personally found to be highly effective.

The Body Keeps Score by Dr. Bessel van der Kolk
If you feel you have any unresolved anxiety, anger, or depression, and this is affecting your parenting, I can't recommend this book enough. Dr. van der Kolk says the problem is unresolved trauma.

Handling Children's Emotions

Between Parent and Child by Dr. Haim Ginott
Liberated Parents, Liberated Children by Adele Faber and Elaine Mazlish
How to Talk so Kids Will Listen by Adele Faber and Elaine Mazlish
If you want more information about how to handle your child's emotions, these are the books to read. The approach in these books, in which children's feelings are treated as valid, was first set forth by Ginott in his book, which has become a classic. Faber and Mazlish were Ginott's students who developed and promoted his ideas. I found Faber and Mazlish's books explain the ideas in a bit more depth and gave me the detail I needed to understand the approach. Ginott's classic however is also excellent.

The Whole-Brain Child by Dr. Daniel Siegel
Along with Ginott, Siegel's is also an excellent book on handling the emotions of the child. The "whole brain" are the parts responsible for logic and emotions. The writing style is very lucid. The book deals somewhat with how to handle trauma, and so any parent dealing with a child who faced trauma is likely to benefit from this book.

Conflict Resolution

Parent Effectiveness Training by Dr. Thomas Gordon
This book outlines an approach to conflict that is negotiation-based instead of authoritarian. The title of this book condescends a bit, as it proposes to make delinquent parents "effective." Many people have been put off by the title. Please see past this. The book is excellent.

Positive Discipline series by Dr. Jane Nelsen et. al
The books in the *Positive Discipline* series are strong in teaching what "tools" work to gain a child's cooperation. The authors also strongly advocate a parenting approach that is non-punitive.

Teaching Young Children

The Montessori Method by Dr. Maria Montessori
To learn how to effectively give lessons to children, I strongly recommend *The Montessori Method* by Dr. Montessori. This is her primary book and it outlines her philosophy of teaching.

Acknowledgments

So many people have mentored me over the years, supported me as I got my parenting blog up and running, and lent their ideas to help create this book. Thank you to Ameeta Saxena, who appears in this book as the "wise woman" and has lent to me her tested and experienced knowledge about young children from her years of working as a Montessori teacher. Thank you to Kelly Elmore, who lends me her wise counsel especially as it relates to conflict resolution and inspired me and continues to inspire me to homeschool. Thank you to Babette Densmore, who has enthusiastically supported my parenting ideas for years now, lends me her own ideas, and whose idea on presenting meals to children appears in this book. Thank you to my former neighbor, Beckie Carpenter, who, as a person in my "normal" life who took notice of my parenting ideas, greatly inspired me to go more public. Thank you to Heather Hutchinson, who supported our family when our children were born and other such emergencies. Thank you to Sunita Sukhraj, Robert Malcom, V Narendra Kumar and many others who have lent me notes of encouragement, asking me to write a book. Thank you to Molly Tietjen, V Narendra Kumar, Sunita Sukhraj, Alexandra LaFontaine, Dr. Michael Garrett, and Ameeta Saxena for serving as beta readers. Many thanks to Keith L Robertson, Babette Densmore, Jessica Blake Thomas McNair, and my husband, Matthew Domoradzki, for lending their editing services. Thank you to John Paquette, who helped me name the sub-title of this book and helped me with many other issues regarding the presentation of material, and to many others who helped me as I worked through particular issues. Thank you to the administrator of the *Beyond the Final Leap* forum, Zoe Brooks, who set up the forum and held the space for this research to be possible. Thank you to the many who contributed to this research, and thank you to those who allowed me to use their quotes which appear in this book. Thank you to the many otherwise strangers to me who saw bits and pieces of my work and took the time to simply tell me they found it accurate, helpful, or inspiring. Thank you to the many others who have taken an interest in my work and this radical notion that "misbehavior is growth." These notes of interest and support really helped as I navigated this difficult process!

Works Cited

Brazelton, T. Berry and Joshua M. Sparrow. Touchpoints--Birth to Three: Your Child's Emotional and Behavioral Development. Second Edition. Cambridge: Da Capo Press, 2006. Kindle Edition.

Ellen Satyr Institute. n.d. Web. 6 October 2017. <http://www.ellynsatterinstitute.org/>.

Faber, Adele and Elaine Mazlish. How to Talk So Kids Will Listen & Listen So Kids Will Talk. New York: Scribner, 2012. Kindle Edition.

—. Liberated Parents, Liberated Children: Your Guide to a Happier Family. Reissue Edition. New York: William Morrow Paperbacks, 2004. Print.

—. Siblings Without Rivalry: How to Help Your Children Live Together So You Can Live Too. New York: W. W. Norton & Company, 2012. Kindle Edition.

Ginott, Haim, Alice Ginott and H. Wallace Goddard. Between Parent and Child: The Bestselling Classic That Revolutionized Parent-Child Communication (Revised and Updated). New York: Three Rivers Press, 2009. Kindle Edition.

Gordon, Thomas. Parent Effectiveness Training: The Proven Program for Raising Responsible Children. New York: Three Rivers Press, 2008. Kindle Edition.

Hart, Cheryle R. and Mary Kay Grossman. The Insulin-Resistance Diet--Revised and Updated: How to Turn Off Your Body's Fat-Making Machine. New York: McGraw-Hill Education, 2008. Kindle Edition.

Hodges, Steve J. It's No Accident: Breakthrough Solutions to Your Child's Wetting, Constipation, UTIs, and Other Potty Problems. Lyons, NY: Lyons Press, 2012. Kindle Edition.

Jones, Wes. Cure Constipation Now: A Doctor's Fiber Therapy to Cleanse and Heal. New York: Berkley Books, 2009. Kindle Edition.

Le Billon, Karen. French Kids Eat Everything: How Our Family Moved to France, Cured Picky Eating, Banned Snacking, and Discovered 10 Simple Rules for Raising Happy, Healthy Eaters. New York: William Morrow, 2012. Kindle Edition.

Margulies, Sheldon. Dr. Sheldon Margulies – Approach to Science Education. n.d. Web. 8 October 2017. <fascinatingeducation.com/>.

Merryman, Ashley. "Losing Is Good for You." New York Times 4 September 2013. Web. 11 October 2017. <www.nytimes.com/2013/09/25/opinion/losing-is-good-for-you.html>.

Montagu, Ashley. Touching: The Human Significance of the Skin. Third edition. New York: Harper & Row, 1986. Print.

Montessori, Maria. Spontaneous Activity in Education. New York: HardPress, 2015. Kindle Edition.

—. The Montessori Elementary Material. Trans. Arthur Livingston. New York: Frederick A. Stokes Company Publishers, 1917. Kindle Edition.

—. The Montessori Method. Blacksburg: EarthAngel Books, 2010. Kindle Edition.

Nelsen, Jane, Cheryl Erwin and Roslyn Ann Duffy. Positive Discipline for Preschoolers: For Their Early Years--Raising Children Who are Responsible, Respectful, and Resourceful. New York: Harmony Books, 2007. Kindle Edition.

—. Positive Discipline: The First Three Years: From Infant to Toddler--Laying the Foundation for Raising a Capable, Confident Child. Completely Revised and Expanded 2nd Edition. New York: Three Rivers Press, 2007. Kindle Edition.

Nelsen, Jane, Lynn Lott and H. Stephen Glenn. Positive Discipline A-Z: 1001 Solutions to Everyday Parenting Problems (Positive Discipline Library). Completely Revised and Expanded Third Edition. New York: Harmony, 2007. Kindle Edition.

Potter-Efron, Ronald. Healing the Angry Brain: How Understanding the Way Your Brain Works Can Help You Control Anger and Aggression. Oakland: New Harbinger Publications, Inc., 2012. Kindle Edition.

Rand, Ayn. "What is Capitalism?" Capitalism: The Unknown Ideal. New York: New American Library, 1966. 11 - 34. Print.

Rosemond, John. Is Your Child Getting Enough Vitamin N? 16 November 2016. Web. 8 October 2017. <www.prageru.com/courses/life-studies/your-child-getting-enough-vitamin-n>.

Rowell, Katja, Jenny McGlothlin and Suzanne Evans Morris. Helping Your Child with Extreme Picky Eating: A Step-by-Step Guide for Overcoming Selective Eating, Food Aversion, and Feeding Disorders. Oakland: New Harbinger Publications, Inc., 2015. Kindle Edition.

Science. n.d. Web. 6 October 2017. <developingchild.harvard.edu/science/>.

Shellenbarger , Sue. "What Teens Need Most From Their Parents: As adolescents navigate the stormiest years in their development, they need coaching, support, good examples and most of all understanding." Wall Street Journal 9 August 2016. Web. 8 October 2017. <www.wsj.com/articles/what-teens-need-most-from-their-parents-1470765906>.

Siegel, Daniel J. and Payne Tina Bryson. The Whole-Brain Child: 12 Revolutionary Strategies to Nurture Your Child's Developing Mind. New York: Delacorte Press, 2011. Kindle Edition.

Stephenson, Susan Mayclin. Child of the World. Arcata: Michael Olaf Montessori Company, 2013. Kindle Edition.

Taranto, James. "The Politicization of Motherhood: Conservatives cheer and liberals jeer New York psychoanalyst Erica Komisar's book on the science of early childhood development." Wall Street Journal 27 October 2017. Web. 3 November 2017. <https://www.wsj.com/articles/the-politicization-of-motherhood-1509144044>.

Thompson, Rob. The Glycemic Load Diet: A Powerful New Program For Losing Weight And Reversing Insulin Resistance. New York: McGraw-Hill, 2012. Kindle Edition.

Tsabary, Shefali. The Awakened Family: A Revolution in Parenting. New York: Viking, 2016. Kindle Edition.

van de Rijt, Hetty and Frans Plooij . The Wonder Weeks: How to stimulate the most important developmental weeks in your baby's first 20 months and turn these 10 predictable, great, fussy phases into magical leaps forward. Trans. Stephen Sonderegger and Gayle Kidder. Arnhem: Kiddy World Promotions B.V., 2012. Kindle Edition.

van der Kolk, Bessel. The Body Keeps Score: Brain, Mind, and Body in the Healing of Trauma. New York: Penguin Books, 2014. Kindle Edition.

White, Burton L. The New First Three Years of Life: The Completely Revised and Updated Edition of the Parenting Classic. New York: Fireside, 1995. Kindle Edition.

About the Author

   Amber Domoradzki has an Industrial Engineering degree from *Penn State University*. She was a software test and integration engineer for 10 years before she decided to become a stay-at-home mother. She has a passion for understanding child development and helping parents. She lives with her husband and three children in "Rocket City"— Huntsville, AL.

Connect With Amber

Website: http://www.TheObservantMom.com

Facebook: https://www.facebook.com/ObservantMom/

Printed in Great Britain
by Amazon

35827152R00119